Bri‹
Joh

Brief Lives:
John Milton

Richard Bradford

Brief Lives
Published by Hesperus Press Limited
28 Mortimer Street, London W1W 7RD
www.hesperuspress.com

First published by Hesperus Press Limited, 2013

Designed and typeset by Fraser Muggeridge studio
Printed in Jordan by Jordan National Press

ISBN: 978-1-84391-926-1

Contents

For Amy Burns

Acknowledgements

Rosemary Savage deserves thanks for her help with this book, and I am grateful also to the University of Ulster. Martha Pooley of Hesperus deserves thanks as a patient and helpful editor. Principal thanks go again to Amy Burns.

Bread Street

William Shakespeare and John Milton are the two most important poets in English. Shakespeare's achievements are unchallengeable and secure. Milton can make a far more controversial claim to eminence. He wrote the only poem in English recognised as an epic, a poem moreover which challenged the beliefs and presuppositions of all of its readers. As a literary writer, his political and historical significance is unique; he was at the centre, involved in, the most traumatic period of modern British history, and this left an imprint on his writings.

The family into which John Milton was born on Friday 9th December 1608 exemplified the mutations and uncertainties of England at the beginning of the seventeenth century. His paternal grandfather, Richard, had been a yeoman and worked a farm near Stanton St John, a village about four miles north of Oxford. Richard had initially occupied a position in the social hierarchy only just above that of the medieval serf but by means still undisclosed, 'probably a good marriage', he acquired an estate that in 1577 was recorded as providing the considerable income of £500 per year.

Milton never made reference to his grandfather in print, which is not entirely surprising given that Richard was also a recusant whose public allegiance to Roman Catholicism earned him excommunication from the Elizabethan Church of England in 1582 and in 1601 fines amounting to £120. Religious difference caused a feud between Richard and his son John, Milton's father. It is known that John senior attended Christ Church, Oxford, sometime during the 1570s, although there is no record of whether he did so as a chorister or a student: he did not receive a degree. In any event it is likely that in Oxford John witnessed the disputations that attended the new theology of Protestantism, then in England barely fifty years old. One day after John had returned to the family home, Richard discovered his son in his room reading that symbolic testament to Anglicanism, the Bible in English. Quarrels between father and son intensified, with the eventual result that in the early 1580s John was disinherited and left Oxfordshire for London, never to return, nor as far as is known to communicate again with Richard.

We do not know how John, then in his early twenties (b. 1562), kept himself when he first arrived in London, but in 1583 or thereabouts he was taken on as an apprentice by James Colbron, a scrivener, and by 1590 had become a successful and independent member of that profession. Scriveners combined the functions of contract lawyer, accountant, financial adviser, money lender and debt collector. They had serviced the guilds and middle-ranking professional classes of the metropolis since the early Middle Ages and by the turn of the sixteenth century they had become, perhaps more than any other profession, the financial beneficiaries of the growing status of London as one of the major trading and seafaring capitals of Europe. John Milton senior did well. By 1600 he felt financially secure enough to court Sara Jeffrey, a woman from a comfortably off family of merchant tailors, whom he married within a year. The marital home would be a five-storey house in Bread Street, near Cheapside, a region favoured by wealthy, upwardly mobile traders and merchants. A street carrying the same name still exists in roughly the same location but all of the properties from the Milton family's time were destroyed in the Great Fire. Their first child died before it could be baptized in May 1601 but a few years later a daughter, christened Anne, survived. John junior later entered the exact details of his own birth in the family Bible: 'the 9th of December 1608 die Veneris [Friday] half an hour after 6 in the morning.' He was baptized in All Hallows parish church, Bread Street on 20th December 1608.

The London into which Milton was born and where he would spend most of his life was undergoing the most radical changes in its history. In 1608 it was effectively two different places. The City itself was an assembly of parishes crowded around the old Gothic St Paul's Cathedral and the Tower, a thriving centre for trade and finance and the obvious location for a scrivener such as Milton senior to base his home and business. Roughly three miles along the curve of the Thames to the west would bring one to Westminster and Whitehall. This was the nation's seat of government, where the monarch held court and the Lords and representatives of the commoners met. Between these two sites there were the Inns of Court, effectively England's third university and devoted entirely to the study of law. Milton's brother Christopher would begin his career as a lawyer at one of the Inns and during his youth Milton himself spent brief periods in residence there, without registering as a student.

Fleet Street and the Strand made up the main highways between Westminster and the City, though our notion of them as urban thoroughfares bears no relation to their character in the early seventeenth century when they were surrounded by what amounted to small palaces and rural estates occupied by the aristocracy and the senior episcopy. To the north of these, the region that we now refer to as the West End, there was little more than lanes and open countryside. Throughout the 1620s and 30s this area became a magnet for England's first wave of property speculators. In 1609 Robert Cecil, Earl of Salisbury, received James's consent to develop a 'Close of fine houses near Leicester Fields' (what is now Leicester Square). Many other similar projects in this region followed and in 1631 Francis Russell, 4th Earl of Bedford, received permission to construct a number of even grander residences in the so-called Covent ('convent') Garden, again north of the Strand. The likely residents would either be members of a growing gentry and aristocracy – both James and Charles were profligate in their conferring of titles and privileges – or those who were amassing wealth from the growing import/export economy based on the river to the east of the City, in what would eventually become London's thriving docklands. Their employees, along with various tradesmen who serviced this expanding metropolis, created an overspill from the City and set themselves up in squalid residences adjacent to the ever expanding squares of the new West End.

The topography of the area altered year by year and it was symbolic of a deeper social and demographic tension. Bedford, for example, was not simply indulging his taste for luxury in his Covent Garden development. His move was tactical. He, like many others in the gentry and aristocracy, was becoming alienated from the court of Charles I. Eventually, the alliance between disaffected gentry and those with interests in the City – individuals like John Milton senior – would make up the power base of the Civil War anti-monarchists. The Bread Street house, where Milton grew up, would have been a spacious, but shapeless, half-timbered structure, each storey being added at various points in its history by a worthy individual with ambitions for more space. The street would have been narrow, crowded and filthy. Drains, as we understand them, did not exist in seventeenth-century London and waste, domestic and human, would lie in these open thoroughfares awaiting heavy, scouring rain. Fresh water, supplied by elm pipes, came at cost shortly after Milton's birth and it is probable that his family would be able to afford this. Milton, from Cambridge onwards, was to cultivate an intense love for the peace and innate beauty of the natural countryside and his upbringing in the crowded dirty city must have played some part in this.

John senior planned for his son a conventional route to success via the educational channels that had been denied to himself. When Milton was ten his father hired for him a private tutor called Thomas Young, a graduate of St Andrews University. Two years later John was admitted to St Paul's School, an esteemed institution adjacent to the Cathedral and only a few minutes' walk from Bread Street. Five years after that, aged sixteen, he would matriculate as an undergraduate at Christ's College, Cambridge, and enjoy the decent status of a 'lesser pensioner', meaning that his father was wealthy enough to pay for modest privileges and accommodation in college.

The influence of these years upon John Milton the writer is undocumented but what we know of them is more than suggestive of their effect. Milton, during the later seventeenth century, was to become the most esteemed and controversial living poet in England, and *Paradise Lost* would remain the poem in English most deserving of the title of epic. His status and reputation were sustained partly by his mastery of language and verse form, but only partly. In his writing he addressed himself to fundamental issues – our relationship with God, our origins, our condition as a species and our fate. These are recurrent features of all Renaissance verse, but Milton had a special, almost unique perspective upon them. He was born into the cauldron of tensions and divisions that characterised English society in the sixteenth and seventeenth centuries, a state which began with Henry VIII's break from the Roman Catholic Church in 1534 and which would reach its apocalyptic climax in the Civil War of the 1640s. Milton not only observed these events, he was a participant in them. He served the republican cause as its most eminent pamphleteer and polemicist during the Civil War years and he would become Latin Secretary – an office not unlike the modern post of a foreign minister – for the victorious Cromwellian governments. No other major English writer has been so closely involved with the intellectual and political shaping of their age. His early years had trained him well for his role and to properly appreciate the nature of this involvement we should broaden the context, allow ourselves a clearer understanding of the world – essentially the religious turbulence which prevailed in England and much of northern Europe – which greeted the arrival of John Milton.

Martin Luther had initiated the Protestant break with Rome, but it was John Calvin, a Geneva theologian, who had created the most radical branch of Protestant theology. His *Institutions of Christian Religion* (1535) became the benchmark for division. In it he proposed a complex theological, indeed philosophical thesis. Essentially, Calvinism was founded upon the tenet of predestination. God has in advance 'elected' those who will be rewarded with eternal, heavenly existence. Human beings enter life in a state of sinfulness, carrying the burden of Adam and Eve's Fall. Therefore we are offered the possibility of redemption, but God has already decided which of us will choose the path to redemption or damnation.

Calvinists maintained the difficult and some would argue paradoxical tenet that (a) we must by our actions redeem ourselves, while; (b) the redeemed have been preselected by God. This troubles us because the original sin of Adam and Eve condemned the human race to a state of punitive detachment from God's wisdom: we must accept even that which we cannot properly understand. Consequently Calvinists argued that the ceremonial rituals of the Roman Church were self-indulgent, even decadent distractions from an attainment even of a limited knowledge of our God-willed condition and fate.

In its early years the English Reformation, particularly during the reign of Henry VIII, was less a theological than a political rebellion; the monarch rather than the pope became the acknowledged head of the church, with all the financial, ideological and legislative benefits carried by that role. The practices of the church itself were largely unaltered by Henry's 1534 Act of Settlement but gradually, through the sixteenth century, more and more Anglicans become apologists and campaigners for what they perceived to be true Protestantism. Influenced by Calvinism they acquired the collective title of 'Puritans'; they sought to purify the Church of England of its Roman practices and beliefs.

As a result there was conflict, evidenced respectively in the reigns of Henry's son Edward VI (1547–53) and daughter Mary I (1553–8). Edward, the so-called boy-king, was pro-Calvinist. He instituted the persecution and execution of Catholics and licensed the radical *Book of Common Prayer* (1549) which for the first time ever offered scripture in vernacular English, an act of independence from predominantly Latinate Roman doctrine. Mary, his sister, went to the other extreme, married Philip II of Spain, a fanatical anti-Protestant, reinstituted Roman Catholicism as the state religion and persecuted radical Protestants. Bishop Latimer and Archbishop of Canterbury Cranmer, both Anglicans with Calvinist sympathies, were burnt at the stake.

The reign of Elizabeth I (1558–1603) restored a degree of compromise. Despite the official re-establishment of an independent Church of England, the nation remained divided, with numerous factions of Protestantism as much set against each other as united in opposition to Catholicism. Elizabeth was obliged to play the role of mediator, which she did with tactical brilliance.

Significantly, the Elizabethan period also involved the emergence of England as a major financial centre. The defeat of the Spanish Armada in 1588 was more than a military / religious victory. English sea power, along with its Dutch counterpart, became the instrument for early colonialism. The West Indies, America and the Indian subcontinent became predominantly English trading centres. The East India Company (referring to the region now comprising the states of India, Sri Lanka, Pakistan and Bangladesh) was founded in 1600, and the 'Company' part of its title reflects the rapidly changing economic condition of London in the later sixteenth century. The establishment of a company whose profits were distributed among shareholders and which was a speculative enterprise was an inaugural feature of modern capitalism. London at the turn of the sixteenth century was alive with companies, and this environment provided Milton's father with a very profitable profession, as what in modern terms would be referred to as an accountant and stockbroker.

These economic transformations were closely related to the ongoing state of religious conflicts: what we now call the middle classes, the traders and entrepreneurs of the period, were predominantly Protestant and Calvinist. And there were a number of reasons for this. Roman Catholicism embodied the feudal, hierarchical systems of medieval Europe and, particularly in England, a new class was emerging, motivated by enterprise and endeavour rather than birthright.

Calvinism did not explicitly incorporate a political philosophy but its conception of man's relationship with God found a sympathetic secular counterpart in the state of mind of the latent middle classes. Calvin emphasised that the elect was an assembly of individuals, unlike the institution of the church with its self-sustaining hierarchies and oppressive conventions. There seemed for many middle-class Protestants to be an obvious parallel between their unsteady relationship with the monarchical, aristocratic structures of the medieval state and with the similarly reactionary characteristics of the old Church, in both its Roman and High Anglican manifestations. But even among Calvinist orientated Protestants there were divisions, caused principally by the notion of predestination. If the elect had already been chosen by God then matters such as conscience in determining an individual's choice between virtuous or sinful acts were at once irrelevant and self-contradictory. The writings of the sixteenth-century Dutch theologian Jacobus Arminius inspired the most divisive feature of Calvinism. Arminius held that the tenet of predestination was flawed – God might well be aware of the choices which would be made by human beings between virtuous and sinful acts but such acts were on our part deliberate. Even though God knew in advance who the elect would be, we, because of our post-lapsarian gift of free will, could still choose our destiny.

The influence of these events upon Milton's beliefs and the course of his life was immense. From his first days at school to his declining years during the Restoration he found himself at the centre of a whirlwind of savagely divided opinions on every aspect of the human condition, from how our faith determined our private demeanour to whether kingship or radical republicanism carried the sanction of God. Some, for the sake of their safety and sanity, might have maintained the lowest possible profile, entering the storm only when obliged to do so. Milton, though never an inflexible zealot, devoted his existence to the defence of what he believed was both God's will and the common good of his countrymen. Opinions on his political and religious views will continue to differ but no one would dispute that his turmoils bequeathed us some of the finest poems ever written.

Arminianist theology did not become the foundation of a particular religious sect or political grouping; rather, it indicates the inherent tensions within the broad spectrum of Protestantism and late Renaissance intellectual life. On the one hand Calvinism replaced attendance to Papal doctrine with an empiricist reading of scripture; at the same time its findings appeared to impose restrictions upon interpretive freedom and the fundamental notion of the believer as a self-determining individual. Arminius reacted against the latter and these doctrinal divisions would be re-enacted within the religious/political fabric of England during the Civil War and its aftermath.

Milton's relationship with Arminianism is important because it operates as an index to his position within and dealings with the complex factionalism of English political and religious life. For example, the term Independents is applied to a large number of prominent individuals of the Parliamentarian cause, Cromwell included. Independency advocated an early version of the modern concept of freedom of the individual, arguing that within the institution of the Protestant church certain particulars of belief should be left to the scrutiny and choice of the individual worshipper. Independency could be regarded as an enactment of Arminianist doctrine, in that both emphasise the importance of choice and self-determination in individuals' dealings with religious practice.

This went against the regimen of the Presbyterian Church, one of the most powerful and influential elements of the Parliamentarian cause. Presbyterianism, originating mainly in Scotland, was organised Calvinism. As an institution it was radical – it rejected the hierarchical Anglican structure of bishops for example – yet authoritarian in that it imposed upon members of its congregation theological ordinances just as unbending as those of the Catholics. As we shall see, the conflicts between Presbyterianism, organised religion and the Independents were continuous during the late 1640s and early 1650s, when the victorious Parliamentarians were restructuring the civic, political and religious fabric of England. Milton, in his early years, sometimes allied himself with aspects of the Calvinist-Presbyterian cause – this was the most emphatically anti-Catholic grouping in Britain – but as he began to establish his reputation as a pamphleteer on religious and political issues and eventually became a civil servant in the Cromwellian republic, he shifted his allegiance to the Independents, the advocates of theological individualism, free speech and free will. Sometimes Milton would attack Arminianism (see *Areopagitica, WJM,* p. 313), not so much as a doctrine in its own right but because it had occasionally, and paradoxically, been adopted by Royalist High Anglicans often as a wedge to further divide the factional constituency of radical Protestantism. Laud, Charles I's notoriously conservative Archbishop of Canterbury, was an advocate of Arminianism but this was more a political tactic than a genuine conviction. He wished to alienate the Presbyterians.

Like many codes of belief, religious and secular, which treat the relation between the conscience of the individual and institutionalised structure in a dialectical, potentially ambiguous manner Arminianism was attractive to otherwise radically opposed parties. In essence, however, it promoted free choice and individualism, and for this reason in much of his later writing Milton supported it (see 'The Ready and Easy Way to Establish a free Commonwealth', 1660, *WJM,* p. 366 and *Of True Religion...,* 1673,

WJM, p. 168). His two most radical and controversial works, the prose tract *De Doctrina Christiana* and the poem *Paradise Lost,* are treated by all commentators as sympathetic to Arminianism: the latter foregrounds the tension between free will and doctrinal obligation by situating it in the lives, thoughts and actions of the two original human beings.

It is certain that even as a child Milton would have become aware of the tensions and polarities of belief that informed all aspects of English politics and religious affiliation. Young, his pre-school tutor, had come to London in the wake of James I's succession to the English throne and would in 1620 take up the post of Pastor of the English church in Hamburg. Young's life in Scotland and his move to Hamburg reflected his Calvinist convictions, and his pupil's lessons in Greek, Latin and Hebrew would have been invested with rather more than a disinterested respect for classical scholarship. Richard Stock, the rector of Milton's parish church, All Hallows, was a Puritan whose Sunday sermons regularly involved the lambasting of Jesuits as the army of Satan and the Pope as their general. Stock had already attained a degree of public notoriety by writing a book in which he claimed that the lax, indulgent nature of the reign of James I had encouraged the return of subversive Papist activists to English life (*A Sermon Preached at Paules Crosse,* 1609). It was licensed for publication two days before John Milton was born. The high master of St Paul's School, Alexander Gill, the surmaster, William Sound and under usher, Alexander Gill junior, all belonged to the more radical wing of the Church of England, and while St Paul's was famous for its emphasis upon classical literature as the bedrock of learning, the writings of Virgil, Cicero, Horace, Homer and Juvenal would all have been examined through the lens of contemporaneous religious doctrine. At St Paul's Milton met Charles Diodati, a boy of his own age who would remain one of his closest friends, and Diodati would have informed him of his family history: his father, a physician, had first been exiled from his native Italy because of his Protestantism, had lived for a while in Geneva, the home of Calvinism, and then moved north to practise his profession in a city, London, in which his religious beliefs would be sympathetically treated; his uncle, Giovanni, had stayed in Geneva to become an influential and controversial theologian, of the Calvinist persuasion.

We cannot be certain of the way the young Milton responded to his early encounters with the prevailing conflicts of the period, but if the writings of the adult are an extension of the inclinations of the child he did not submit to indoctrination. He would throughout his life remain a radical Protestant, but Milton's radicalism was of the non-peremptory, undogmatic kind. The features of Calvinism that corresponded most with his temperament were the concepts of individualism and free will, God's generous allocation to his fallen species of the opportunity to speculate on the nature of absolute truth before accepting a pre-formed actuality.

At St Paul's an attainment of competence in Greek and Latin was regarded as of equal importance to a pupil's mastery of his native English, and a knowledge of the poetic conventions of all three languages was ranked almost as highly as a command of their grammar. Pupils were asked to write poems, not as vehicles for expressive creativity but as exercises of self-discipline; a practical awareness of metre and figurative devices inculcated a greater understanding of linguistic operations per se. This ranking of poetry as an intrinsic feature of language, rather than as a self-conscious excursion from its ordinary uses, reflects its broader status within Renaissance culture. Gill senior was a quintessential Renaissance schoolteacher in that he treated Greek, Latin and English as living languages whose interrelationships were mutually productive. He informed his pupils of the relative qualities of contemporary English poets, of how they had adapted, transformed and extended the precedents set by their classical precursors: Spenser was 'our Homer', Sidney was the English Anacreon, Samuel Daniel the modern Lucan and John Harington the Elizabethan Martial. Shakespeare, as a playwright, was in Gill's opinion a little too populist for serious scrutiny. (see Parker, p. 14).

At home poetry was treated as a necessary feature of the civilised household. His father, despite lacking a formal education, was an enthusiastic poet. He was a close friend of John Lane, an editor and publisher of verse and himself a writer, albeit of questionable competence. Milton senior set a number of psalms to music and contributed poems to several of Lane's collections (see Parker, p. 16). Milton's father's verse reminds one of William McGonagall's late nineteenth-century combination of disarming sincerity and embarrassing ineptitude. Milton's opinions upon his father's poems are a matter for speculation and one is tempted to wonder if they encouraged an early regard for stylistic probity. Milton himself certainly wrote verse during this period. Undated epigrams on the Gunpowder Plot survive, along with exercises in Latin elegiac verse, but they could have been produced by anyone; Milton the poet would not find his individual voice, at least in English, until he was in his twenties.

Cambridge

Milton, just sixteen, arrived in Christ's College, Cambridge on 12th February 1625 and he matriculated on 9th April. It is more than likely that Milton was conveyed between Cambridge and London by Thames Hobson, who made the journey with his own carriage once a week and rented horses or drawn carriages to students when they required transportation more urgently. Milton certainly remembered him. Shortly after Hobson's death in 1631 he wrote a poem called 'On the University Carrier'. It is a mock-heroic piece which does not exactly satirise Hobson but treats him more as a subject for amused curiosity than with respect.

> *Merely to drive the time away he sickened,*
> *Fainted, and died, nor would with ale be quickened,*
> *Nay, quoth he, on his swooning be outstretched,*
> *If I may not carry, sure I'll ne'er be fetched.*
>
> (16–19)

We tend to date the quintessentially English tendency toward class consciousness and snobbery to the nineteenth century but Milton's patronizing tribute to Hobson causes us to question that. Perhaps Milton's time at Christ's encouraged a feeling of superiority. The college itself was not the grandest in Cambridge – Trinity and King's paraded their wealth and eminence with ostentatiously expensive buildings – but it carried an air of the modest country house. Its buildings were distributed across what were once open fields which had by Milton's arrival become mature, planned gardens, now known as Christ's Piece. The gardens also included an orchard and an enclosed tennis court, and to the west of the college its members could walk along the banks of the Cam. Its buildings were shared, on average, by 250 students and more than 20 fellows all of whom lodged in generously spaced rooms in the two-storey quadrangles. The day at Christ's began at five with morning service in the college chapel. Breakfast would follow in Hall between six and seven and the rest of the morning involved disputations between students and their tutors, the origin of the modern-day tutorial, and lectures either in the Public Schools or in college. Dinner, the main meal of the day, was taken at noon and during the afternoon students, unless required for specific disputations, were left largely to themselves. Recreation during these hours took the form of games of tennis, fencing, bathing in the Cam or wrestling. Some, if from wealthy enough backgrounds, would stable horses in the town and ride during their spare time. Regulations stated that undergraduates must be accompanied by dons when they ventured beyond the gates of the college but few if any had the time or inclination to observe this rule. We cannot be certain of how Milton occupied his free hours but he later insisted that he was an adept swordsman, so it is possible that he acquired this skill at Cambridge. 'When he was Young' claims Richardson, 'he learnt to Fence, probably as a Gentlemanly Accomplishment, and that he might be Able to do Himself Right in Case of an Affront' (Darbishire, p. 204). Just as likely, the vast acres of open land surrounding the colleges encouraged his enduring love of walking in the countryside. After vespers, supper would be taken at seven and unless they had a special dispensation no one was allowed out of college after nine o'clock.

His friend Diodati had gone up to Oxford two years earlier and it is likely that the Miltons chose Cambridge because of its reputation as generally more sympathetic to the cause of radical

Protestantism. University dons were mostly clergymen, but if Milton had expected to join a community which addressed itself to the theological and political controversies of the day he was to be very disappointed. His Cambridge experiences, of which in any event there are few reliable records, can best be described as dull. He made no close friends there; the curriculum, unchanged for several hundred years, involved the standard retinue of rhetoric, logic and ethics, with a smattering of Greek and mathematics (Latin was the language of instruction). Speculation and open argument during disputations were frowned upon, and inculcation preferred. If the move from school to university involved the expectation of a shift from regimentation to intellectual challenge, this for Milton seemed to have gone into reverse. St Paul's had offered a far more stimulating, unorthodox environment than his new home.

Christ's might have conformed to the educational regime of the rest of the university but another aspect of its milieu contributed to the one notable occurrence during Milton's time there as a student, his temporary expulsion from the university in the Spring Term of 1626. Most of the fellows and students were advocates of various aspects of Calvinism and Puritanism and by the time Milton arrived Christ's, along with Emmanuel and Sidney Sussex, was becoming an outpost of resistance to the High Anglicanism that had taken root in much of the rest of the university. Milton's younger brother Christopher would many years later tell of how John had, after disagreements with his tutor William Chappell, 'received some unkindness'. Speculative biographers subsequently assumed that this had meant that he had been 'sent down' from the university as a punishment for insubordination and such assumptions are based upon a poem in Latin by Milton himself called 'Elegia prima ad Carlolum Diodati' ('Elegy I to Charles Diodati') a versified letter to his friend – they corresponded regularly and always in Latin – which includes references to his college rooms as 'forbidden', and to his 'exile' and 'banishment'.

Whatever the exact nature of the event – and Christopher also refers to Chappell as having 'whip't him [contrary to] ye Rules of ye College' – what is known is that Chappell had a reputation as a formidable intellectual disciplinarian and unyielding debater, having once reduced James I to virtual silence during a University Assembly. He was also an intractable Arminianist, unwilling even to countenance the possibility of any other theological principle. As has been made clear, Milton too would come to champion the Arminianist emphasis upon free will and the power of conscience but it is likely that he took against a man who exemplified theological totalitarianism, even if he shared his interpretation of scripture. The fact that on his return Milton was assigned a different tutor, Nathaniel Tovey, reinforces the suspicions of a temperamental antipathy between him and Chappell, as does the poem to Diodati on his 'exile' to London. 'I am not pining away for any rooms... I do not like having always to stomach the threats of a stern tutor and other things which my spirit will not tolerate' (II, 12–16, translated from the original Latin into English prose).

Aside from the poem we cannot be certain of what exactly Milton did during his time away from the university, yet so rhapsodic is his portrayal of what amounts to his first period of independence that one begins to wonder about its authenticity. He speaks of 'how badly that place [Cambridge] suits the worshippers of Phoebus!' and tells of his days walking in the countryside just beyond the City of London, of his new-found enjoyment of the theatre, of the vibrancy of the streets, and writes almost in wonder at the visions of womanhood abroad in the metropolis, as if he had encountered real members of the opposite sex for the first time. Does he protest too much? The fact that the poem is in Latin might seem of no great significance since it would have been standard for Milton and Diodati to advertise their mutual respect as able practitioners of the language and its poetic conventions, but it seems not accidental that it was also a suitable vehicle for his presentation of experiences that might have been borrowed from any number of classical poems celebrating the joys of bucolic, social and literary life. And, despite numerous attempts during the Renaissance to reconcile classical culture and learning with Christianity, the former remained doggedly pre-Christian. Perhaps Milton was creating for himself, and Diodati, a fantasy world in which the pressures and conflicts of Cambridge, which exemplified those of England as a whole, might be suspended.

Apart from a few revisions of psalms the only poems in English by Milton before he received his Bachelor of Arts degree in 1629 were 'On the Death of An Infant Dying of a Cough' and 'At a Vacation Exercise in College'. Both are skilled and competent pieces of work, yet as the latter suggests they read more as exercises than as confident poetic statements. The 'Elegia' to Diodati on the other hand is a precocious, masterly blend of technical refinement and candid informality. Latin seemed to be the medium in which the teenage Milton felt most comfortable. It was the principal language of intellectual and theological debate, reliable and established; while English, like England, appeared to incorporate unease and uncertainty.

In February 1626 Charles I was crowned at Westminster Abbey. His predecessor James I (crowned 1604) had attempted to maintain Elizabeth's balance between religious radicalism and conservatism, and with a degree of success. But for various reasons – including the fact that James had previously been king of Scotland and had brought with him to London many Calvinist advocates of Scottish Presbyterianism – division still continued in England. Little was known of Charles's intentions but it soon became evident to those close to the centre of power that the new monarch lacked the intellectual and tactical acumen of his two predecessors and that the traditionalist rather than the Puritan wing of the Church of England was gaining ground. For example, it would have been customary for the Dean of Westminster, John Williams, to have officiated at the coronation but Williams was known to sympathise with the more radical elements of Anglicanism. He was mysteriously absent, his place being taken by William Laud, then Bishop of Bath and Wells, who favoured the practice of Catholic rites and who would eventually become Archbishop of Canterbury and a fervent supporter of the Royalist cause during the Civil War.

As the episode with Chappell suggests, there is evidence that Milton maintained an informed awareness of contemporary religious and political developments. Indeed during 1626 Cambridge itself became the stage for a series of events which reflected the ongoing tensions of London. Two candidates stood for the post of Chancellor of the University: George Villiers, Duke of Buckingham enjoyed the explicit support of the king, while Thomas Howard, Earl of Berkshire was promoted by the House of Commons. Effectively, it was High Anglicanism versus Puritanism. Chancellors were elected by fellows of colleges and Buckingham won by a very slight majority. The Commons suspected royal intrigue and vote rigging, demanded the suspension of Buckingham, and Charles, in response, prorogued Parliament on 26th June. It was as though the early scenes of the Civil War were being rehearsed in the halls of academe.

Milton would have witnessed these events – the election was the subject of public debate throughout the university – and a Latin poem written a few months later in early 1627, as a letter to his ex-tutor Thomas Young, shows that he knew and thought a great deal about closely related matters. In 'Elegia Quarta' he presents Hamburg, where Young was still Pastor of the English church, as a city under siege by the pro-Catholic armies of the ongoing Thirty Years War. (In military terms it was not, but its reputation as a centre for Lutheran Protestantism offered evidence of its symbolic status as a bastion.) In the poem he addresses Young as a tragic exemplar of the true religion who like many others has been forced to flee to the solidly Protestant enclaves of Europe or New England.

Milton, in April 1629, was awarded his Bachelor of Arts degree. With his new tutor, Nathaniel Tovey, he had worked hard and acquired a qualification which was the equivalent, in modern classification, of a borderline First. He decided to stay on and do a Master's degree. Why exactly Milton chose to continue with a regime of intensive study is not known; what is, is that, on Christmas Day 1629, he began what would be his first significant poem in English, 'On the Morning of Christ's Nativity'. Poems celebrating holy days were a customary feature of Renaissance culture, but what is striking about this one is a sense of intellectual presence which carries it beyond standard expectations of a respectful poeticisation of the birth of Christ. He virtually challenges the reader to engage with the gigantic complexity of the event. It set a precedent for verse that would follow, and introduced Milton as a figure for whom poetry, while attending to its aesthetic obligations, was a vehicle for contention, exposition and ratiocination.

The political and theological issues of Milton's early years would play their part in his subsequent writing and thinking, but what of the role of contemporary poetry?

Shakespeare was still alive during Milton's early childhood and the Mermaid Tavern, where Ben Jonson and other writers with a taste for drink held their 'merry meetings', was a few hundred yards from Bread Street. In 1621 John Donne, then aged forty-nine, became Dean of St Paul's and Milton, as a pupil at the Cathedral school, would have heard him preach. Donne's verse would not appear in print until 1633, shortly after his death, but manuscript copies were in circulation among poetry enthusiasts of the day and it is almost certain that these would have passed through the Bread Street household. It is therefore both intriguing and puzzling that Donne and his work feature neither in Milton's writings nor in records of his opinions.

Twentieth-century consensus esteemed Donne as the archetype of a school of writing, predominant in England during the early seventeenth century, known as Metaphysical Poetry. Samuel Johnson in his *Lives of the Poets* (1779) offered a concise description of the Metaphysicals' technique; in their verse 'heterogeneous ideas are yoked by violence together'. Johnson was referring, albeit disapprovingly, to the so-called conceit, a metaphor which emphasises and frequently does not attempt to resolve the paradoxical relationship between two ideas, perceptions or states of mind. T.S. Eliot in a 1921 essay on the Metaphysicals offered a single line from Donne's 'The Relic' as an example of this: 'A bracelet of bright hair about the bone'. The bone referred to is the wrist of a man's skeleton, uncovered many years after burial but still bearing the thread of a woman's hair as a token of his endless love for her. Into eight words Donne has compressed a catalogue of opposing concepts: life as temporary versus love as timeless; physical decay versus imperishable beauty; a decorative token versus eternal commitment, etc.

Other poets of the period whose work involved the frequent use of the adventurous conceit were George Herbert (1593–1633) and Andrew Marvell (1621–78). As these dates indicate, several of the writers who would later be classified as belonging to the Metaphysical School were near contemporaries of Milton – indeed Marvell would become his colleague and close friend. As a young man, when evolving his own perceptions of English poetry, Milton would have been aware of the writings of the first generation of the Metaphysicals, particularly those of Donne and Herbert (Herbert, incidentally, was University Orator during Milton's first few years at Cambridge), but we know practically nothing of what he thought of them. Parker, Milton's biographer, writes that 'London was not so large that a young poet found it impossible to meet the masters of his art if he desired to do so. Milton, unfortunately, left us no account of such meetings' (p. 61).

A number of questions are raised by Milton's apparent reluctance to address himself to contemporary verse. Did he, as a classicist, regard the Greek and Latin poets as innately superior to their English-language counterparts? If that were the case then why did he also begin to write verse in English? Another possibility is suggested by the thesis and indeed the title of a book by the modern critic Harold Bloom, *The Anxiety of Influence* (1973), in which Bloom argues that many aspiring poets are so convinced of their own uniqueness that they set about detaching them-selves from the reputations of both their precursors and their contemporaries. The only occasion on which Milton did refer in print to another major English poet was in a short poem called 'On Shakespeare', written in Cambridge in 1630 and printed in 1632 among prefatory material to the Shakespeare Second Folio. Shakespeare had been dead for fourteen years when Milton wrote the poem and it was already becoming evident that his enduring genius would outstrip his contemporaneous popularity. Milton's poem is at once diligently respectful and unnerving, in that he addressed it not so much to Shakespeare the man as to his work which, he implies, is of far more significance than his living presence.

There is one couplet which is particularly unsettling:

> *Then thou our fancy of itself bereaving,*
> *Dost make us marble with too much conceiving*

Here Milton seems to be, with polite ambiguity, suggesting that the influence of Shakespeare, or at least his work, could be counterproductive. Milton implies that 'too much conceiving' (the overuse of extravagant metaphor) will consign poets to the past ('make us marble') rather than cause them to endure via their work. Is he suggesting that Shakespeare's surpassing skill with figurative language has become both his monument and, more sadly, the self-indulgent inheritance of his successors, the Metaphysicals? 'On the Morning of Christ's Nativity' makes it clear that Milton regarded poetry more as a vehicle for the clarification of essential notions of the human condition than, as he implied of Shakespeare, an excuse for performing tricks with language.

He does not alter the detail of the Biblical story, but the feature of the poem which has maintained its accredited significance is its tendency to cause the reader to think closely about the very notion of God's incarnation, the intersection of the timeless and ineffable with the transient and fragile state of mortality.

In Stanza 14 he evokes the effect of the angelic choir:

For if such holy song
Enwrap our fancy long,
Time will run back and fetch the age of gold,
And speckled vanity
Will sicken soon and die,
And lep'rous sin will melt from earthly mould,
And hell itself will pass away,
And leave her dolorous mansions to the peering day.

(133–40)

This and the stanza following it are ambiguously optimistic. The birth of Christ seems to offer a relatively painless and generous form of redemption. Sin, hell, mortality ('the dolorous mansions' and 'the peering day') are briefly removed; humanity seems to have been returned to 'the age of gold'. But as we should be aware, this age, our prelapsarian state, is irretrievable, and in Stanza 16 Milton reminds us of the fact.

But wisest fate says no
This must not yet be so.

(149–50)

The child in the manger must be crucified:

The babe lies yet in smiling infancy,
That on the bitter cross
Must redeem our loss.

(151–3)

This concertinaing of Christ's life, most specifically the image of a crucified infant, is deliberately shocking. The effect of the image underpins Milton's message – before we can return to a golden age, comparable to the time before the Fall, there is much suffering to be done, by Christ and us.

Throughout the poem Milton interweaves his presentation of the events attending the birth of Christ with intimations of theological truths that underpin it. In the first two stanzas he notes that

Nature in awe to him
Had doffed her gaudy trim

(32–3)

Nature has chosen to 'hide her guilty front with innocent snow', has thrown 'the saintly veil of maiden white' upon her 'foul deformities'. Later in Stanza 7 he returns to this theme and tells how the sun

Hid his head for shame
As his inferior flame
The new enlightened world no more should need.

(80–2)

The natural world was presented frequently in Renaissance verse as an approximation of its Edenic counterpart, its beauty a part of God's design, but Milton turns this strategy around and reminds the reader that nature, incorporating man, is an element of our post-lapsarian state. Its attractions are but 'foul deformities' compared with what we have lost and appropriately it hides itself from the coming of Christ.

The poem is striking in that it continually projects its ostensible topic into a broader, all-inclusive contemplation of man's relationship with God, focusing particularly upon the reason for the coming of Christ – man's original act of disobedience and its consequences. Again, we should note that while this was an ever-present feature of Renaissance, post-Reformation consciousness, its emphatic resurfacing in Milton's early verse suggests that as a poet he had an agenda, a scale of priorities. And he would eventually address himself directly to its apex: *Paradise Lost*, the fall of man.

It is evident from Milton's early poetry that he was as confident and skilled in his use of figurative devices as any of his contemporaries, but it is equally clear that, unlike most of the Metaphysicals, he used language, poetic language, as a means of logically addressing the uncertainties of life, unlocking them; not as an experiment but as a harsh confrontation with the relation between language and knowledge.

Two other poems, written in 1631, during Milton's final year at Cambridge, attest to his growing perception of poetry as a vehicle for both creative and intellectual endeavour. 'L'Allegro' and 'Il Penseroso' are poetic versions of the academic debating exercise where one person displays his skill as a rhetorician by arguing the relative values of two opposing, sometimes antithetical, ideas or propositions. Milton was required to do this as part of his Master's degree and the two poems are based upon his engagement with the question of 'Whether Day or Night is More Excellent'. The principal criterion for success in this academic exercise involved the extent to which equanimity and balance could be achieved between the opposing perspectives, and Milton's poetic celebration of the various joys, benefits and opportunities of daytime and night-time experience attempts a similar exercise in symmetry. There is, however, a slight but detectable sense of empathy and commitment in 'Il Penseroso' (the night poem), while 'L'Allegro' (the day poem) involves more of an exercise in allegiance. In short, Milton discloses himself to be more innately predisposed to a state of mind which is removed from the distractions of unreflecting pleasure – he prefers night to day.

For example, two lines in 'L'Allegro' have exercised the attentions of numerous commentators:

Then to come in spite of sorrow
And at my window bid good morrow

(46–7)

No one has been able to demonstrate precisely who or what comes to the window. It might be the mountain nymph (referred to in line 36), the singing lark (line 41) or Milton himself. The most likely explanation for this case of loose ambiguous syntax – very uncommon in a young man so alert to the discipline of composition – was that Milton in this poem was performing a duty, listing the pleasures of the day in the manner of a filing clerk, without any real enthusiasm or private enjoyment. As a consequence his attention lapses and he offers up a lazily constructed sentence.

Try as he might Milton cannot quite prevent elements of his temperamental disposition from disrupting the exercise in balance supposedly enacted in the two poems. At the conclusion of 'Il Penseroso' he asks night-time to

Dissolve me into ecstasies
And bring all heaven before mine eyes

(165–6)

implying that only the inner eye, the contemplative state, can enable human beings to properly understand what lies beyond the given world. In 'L'Allegro' he celebrates the pleasure of daytime as

Such sights as youthful poets dream
On summer eves by haunted stream

(129–30)

and one should note that these sights inspire 'youthful' poets, implying that their more mature counterparts have moved beyond such distractions to thought.

The closing couplets of both poems are intriguing. The one

from 'L'Allegro' is conditional:

> *These delights, if those can'st give,*
> *Mirth with thee, I mean to live.*

(151–2)

This suggests, subtly, that he could live with Mirth, if only… Compare this with the certainty of 'Il Penseroso':

> *These pleasures Melancholy give,*
> *And I with thee will choose to live.*

(175–6)

These poems are important because they cause us to look beyond them to more emphatic disclosures of Milton's state of mind in later work. They re-address a theme raised in the 'Nativity Ode', where the diversions and attractions of the known world are temporarily suspended for the birth of Christ. Milton would eventually go blind and his sonnet on this condition recaptures the mood of 'Il Penseroso'; the contemplative, unseeing state is now an obligation, not a choice, and it seems to suit his temperament. More significantly, in the so-called 'Address to Light' at the beginning of Book III of *Paradise Lost*, Milton revisits 'Il Penseroso'. He is about to bring God into a poem and the lines on how darkness might 'bring all heaven before mine eyes' written thirty years before must surely have registered for the now blind poet.

Shortly before Milton's departure from Cambridge his father created what turns out to be our first record of his adult appearance and demeanour. John senior, prompted perhaps by his son's growing reputation as a poet, commissioned a portrait of him for which he sat during the weeks after his twenty-first birthday. The Puritan fashion for short pudding-bowl haircuts was not quite as widespread in 1630 as it would be during the Civil War but it was already worn by many as a sign of allegiance. Milton's wavy brown hair falls to his collar. His black doublet and white falling ruff is the unashamed costume of a gentleman. Toland, who based his biography on accounts from Milton's friends and family, describes him in a manner that complements the portrait well: 'he made a considerable figure... He was middlesiz'd and well proportion'd, his Deportment erect and manly, his Hair of a light brown, his Features exactly regular, his Complexion wonderfully fair as a Youth, and ruddy to the last' (Darbishire, pp. 193–4).

Reflection

After seven years at Cambridge (1625–32), there were several career paths open to Milton. In 1631, his younger brother Christopher had been admitted to the Inner Temple in London to study for the profession of lawyer, but it had been assumed that John would make use of his considerable academic achievements and enter the more respectable sphere of the church. Instead he chose an existence that some might regard as self-indulgent. He would spend the next seven years reading, thinking, writing and travelling.

In the autumn of 1631 Milton's father retired from business, gave up the house in Bread Street and moved with his wife Sara to Hammersmith, now part of Greater London but then a quiet country village some seven miles from the City. Less than a year later his son took up residence with him to begin what amounted to an extended period of self-education. As he would later reflect, 'At my father's house in the country, to which he had gone to pass his old age, I gave myself up with the most complete leisure to reading through the Greek and Latin writers; with the proviso, however, that I occasionally exchanged the country for the town, for the sake of buying books or of learning something new in mathematics or music, in which I then delighted' (*WJM*, VII, p. 120). There is a sense here of Milton attending at once to the orthodoxies of intellectual endeavour, particularly classical learning, while calculatedly removing himself from the demands and opportunities of the contemporary world. He seemed set upon an objective, but its exact nature and the manner of its realisation remained undisclosed. There were, however, indications.

The most revealing account of what Milton was attempting to achieve during those years of retirement came from the man himself in a 1633 letter to an unidentified correspondent (the fact that the letter is in English, rather than Latin, and that its manner is formal rather than intimate, discount Diodati as the recipient). He confesses that the 'sin of curiosity…' is causing him to become 'the most helplesse, pusilanimous and unweapon'd creature'. He reflects upon the various options of an active life – marriage, the routine professions of the moneyed classes – and by his tone betrays a disinclination towards any of them, bordering upon fecklessness.

> There is against yt [his supposed inclination to the retired life] a much more potent inclination imbred which about this tyme of a mans life solicits most, the desire of house & family of his owne to which nothing is esteemed more helpefull then the early entering into credible employment… and though this were anough yet there is to this another act if not of pure, yet of refined nature no lesse available to dissuade prolonged obscurity, a desire of honour & repute, & immortall fame seated in the brest of every true scholar which all make hast to by the readiest ways of publishing & divulging conceived merits as well those that shall as those that never shall obtaine it.

> (*CPW*, I, pp. 319–20)

Regarding the ministry, he refers to the parable of the talents,

> from due & timely obedience to that command in the gospell set out by the terrible seasing of him that hid the talent. it is more probable therefore that not the endless delight of speculation but this very consideration of that

great commandment does not presse forward as soone as
may be to underg[o] but keeps off with a sacred reverence
& religious advisement how best to undergoe[,] not taking
thought of being late so it give advantage to be more fit.

(CPW, I, p. 320)

He appears here to be ransacking the Gospels for some pretext
that would justify his decision to remain in a state of limbo. To
become a clergyman, indeed even to partake of the ceremony
of marriage, would mean that he would have to declare some
degree of affiliation to a faction of the Protestant faith, and the
latter was becoming more splintered by the month. To some,
this might seem a strategy of avoidance yet there is evidence to
suggest that he had chosen to observe events from a distance,
consider what he witnessed in relation to his private regime of
reading, and wait upon the day that the sum of his wisdom might
be employed as a calling or vocation.

Milton would already have witnessed at Cambridge the
growing tensions between the advocates of Puritanism and the
better-established champions of High Anglicanism. In the university, theology was still largely a matter for abstract speculation and private commitment but within England as a whole
these same divisions were coming to influence conventions gov-
erning behaviour and lifestyle. The Puritan position was made
clear in William Prynne's *Histrio-Mastix: or, The Players Scourge
and Actors Tragedy* (1632). As indicated by his title Prynne was
particularly agitated by stage plays and masques, which he saw
as licensing hedonism and immorality, but this was but his opening tirade in a thousand-page invective against dancing, may-
poles, sports of any kind, rural fairs, stained glass windows,
ostentatiously decorated altars, the wearing of garishly coloured
vestments by members of the clergy and much more. Prynne's
logic is clear enough: there is a causal relationship between
secular activities in which display or enjoyment are prominent
and religious practices that show allegiances to Catholicism.

Prynne and many other extremist Puritans held that indulgent gratification was not only immoral but an indication of treacherous affiliations to enemies of England, specifically the Catholic nations of continental Europe.

Prynne's book was prompted by a tendency in Charles's court to sponsor plays and masques which celebrated him and Queen Henrietta as at once passionate yet ungoverned by the rules thought appropriate for fallen humanity. Moreover Charles attempted to promulgate the culture of his court to the nation as a whole. Throughout the early 1630s he issued proclamations commanding gentry and nobility to run their country estates as hospitable sinecures in which the lower orders would be encouraged, with financial sponsorships, to treat the Sabbath and other holidays as the opportunity for relaxation and recreation. Indeed as a direct rebuke to Prynne's polemic Charles ordered to be reissued in 1633 a revised edition of James I's controversial *Book of Sports*. According to this, on Sundays 'our good people be not disturbed, letted or discouraged from any lawful recreation, such as dancing, either men or women; archery for men, leaping, vaulting, or any other such harmless recreation, nor from having of May-games, whitsunales, and Morris-dances; and the setting up of May-Poles and other sports therewith used.'

During that same year Laud became Archbishop of Canterbury and immediately began to bring the church into line with his own high Anglican beliefs and practices, ordering his bishops to supervise closely what was preached and what rituals performed. Puritan-leaning ministers would be ejected and forbidden from setting up private chaplaincies. Ordinances were issued requiring fixed altars to replace plain communion tables and clergy were told to conduct services in vestments that were virtually identical to those of Catholic priests. It is certain that Milton was aware of this. Even if his self-imposed country exile detached him from the cauldron of dispute that was London he would need only to attend his local parish church to witness the changes. While he showed reluctance to comment directly on contemporary events it is clear from his poetry in this period that such matters were exercising his imagination.

Close to the Milton house was the estate of Harefield, presided over by Alice, Countess of Derby. Milton was introduced to the household by Henry Lawes, a composer and musician, who had been a friend of his father's since the Bread Street days. Lawes, at the time, was music teacher to the Countess's grandchildren. Milton's attachment to the household is celebrated in his 1633 piece 'Arcades'. 'Arcades' began as a masque, a brief drama involving verse, music and scenic effects, in which the Duchess is presented as the matriarch of a rural paradise in which the arts flourish. (Countess Derby, then aged seventy-two, had been a well-known patron of poets and playwrights, Spenser included.) But the work is more than a gift to his patroness. In the middle of the piece Milton introduces the 'celestial sirens' (63), figures borrowed from Plato's *Republic* whose voices harmonise the concentric whorls of the universe, and blends this image with his by now familiar notion of

the heavenly tune, which none can hear
Of human mould with gross unpurged ear
(*TP*: 72–3)

This, like the music which accompanies the birth of Christ in the 'Nativity Ode', is an expression of God's presence from which the Fall has detached human beings.

The most interesting section of 'Arcades' is the conclusion of the Genius's address (74–84), in which Milton finds himself having to reconcile the notion of music which is beyond human comprehension with the newly elevated, almost otherworldly, status of the Dowager. To have caused her to hear it would have been both sacrilegious and sycophantic, and Milton provides a deftly evasive compromise: '[S]uch music' would be worthy of 'her immortal praise' if only 'my [Milton's] inferior hand or voice could hit/Inimitable sounds' (75–8). The 'heavenly tone' would indeed be a fitting tribute to her status, but she is attended by lowly human beings who cannot produce it.

While this might seem to ally him with the Court-sponsored forms of entertainment so decried by the Puritans he subtly incorporates a meditation on the timeless notion of spirituality and the limitations of the ordinary human state. He was, demonstrably, answering questions raised by his refusal to commit himself to a career. Tentatively, he was finding in poetry a means of exploring the controversies that would soon drive England into warring factions.

In June 1631 the Earl of Bridgewater, the Countess's son-in-law, was appointed Lord Lieutenant of Wales, and Lawes and Milton decided to collaborate in the writing of his second masque to celebrate this. 'A Masque Presented at Ludlow Castle', later to be known as *Comus*, was first performed in September 1634 in the grounds of Ludlow, one of Bridgewater's official residences. Lawes wrote the music for the song parts, and the words, sung and spoken, were Milton's. Three of the parts would be played by Bridgewater's children, who, as Lawes' pupils, had been well prepared for the demands of acting and singing.

The uncomplicated plot centres upon the kidnapping by the eponymous Comus, a semi-human demonic presence, of The Lady (played by the fifteen-year-old Lady Alice), whom he then attempts to seduce. It is a fairy story involving a conflict between Virtue and Vice; the former triumphs and a joyous, idyllic mood prevails. *Comus* was designed as the centrepiece of an evening of dancing and restrained conviviality; it was intended to reflect for its audience, and its participants, a collective feeling of familial order and optimism. (The Lady is eventually rescued by her two brothers, played by Lady Alice's brothers, John and Thomas.) Milton, who was responsible for the script and the direction of the plot, wraps a moral fable in light and decorative poetic dress, but at the same time, particularly during the verbal struggle between Comus and The Lady, he inscribes a more disturbing subtext – something that would have resonated for the adult, informed members of the audience.

Three years earlier, in 1631, Countess Derby's other son-in-law, Lord Castlehaven, had been at the centre of a trial which, if tabloid newspapers had existed at the time, would have become the newsprint scandal of the decade. Castlehaven was a bisexual, a paedophile and a sadist. He obliged a number of his male servants to have sex with him and on several occasions forced one of them, called Skipwith, to rape Castlehaven's twelve-year-old stepdaughter Elizabeth, an act in which he was both spectator and participant. Castlehaven was found guilty and executed in May 1631.

The family would have recognised the parallels – an adult, demonic figure of aristocratic bearing attempts to satiate himself with a virgin child. Comus, unlike Castlehaven, fails, but there was an implied postscript. Castlehaven was a Roman Catholic and an enthusiastic supporter of Charles I. Prynne in *Histrio-Mastix* cites Castlehaven as the worst exemplar of his religious creed, and from this he argues that the grand ceremonialism of the Roman Church encourages the most sinful, lewd, pernicious aspects of our fallen condition. For virtually everyone who witnessed the performance of the masque the curious intersections between the Castlehaven case and the broader polemical sweep of Prynne's book would have been evident. Milton was harnessing his talents as a poet to a more solemn commitment, involving fundamental elements of belief and behaviour. His seemingly self-indulgent period of withdrawal was in truth quite the opposite.

The most important section of *Comus* is lines 558–812, in which The Lady is 'set in' and apparently unable to remove herself from 'an enchanted chair'. The section is a dialogue between The Lady and Comus, who appears to have entrapped her in a fantastic, enchanted realm. Comus is attempting to seduce her and the following are examples of his rhetorical technique:

> *If all the world*
> *Should in a pet of temperance feed on pulse,*
> *Drink the clear stream, and nothing wear by frieze,*
> *The All-giver would be unthanked, would be unpraised,*
> *Not half his riches known, and yet despised.*

(719–23)

> *Beauty is nature's coin, must not be hoarded,*
> *But must be current, and the good thereof*
> *Consists in mutual and partaken bliss,*
> *Unsavoury in the enjoyment of itself.*
> *If you let slip time, like a neglected rose*
> *It withers on the stalk with languished head.*

(738–43)

The passages are significant because they transcend their immediate context and involve Milton in an engagement with contemporary poetic and social conventions. They invite comparison with the amatory mode of Metaphysical poetry in which the male speaker makes use of his considerable stylistic and referential abilities to persuade the female listener of something; frequently that sex with him is entirely consistent with God's design for the universe and the status of human beings within it. Comus argues that nakedness is God's gift and that he would be 'unthanked' if it were not fully appreciated and indeed made use of 'in mutual and partaken bliss'. Beauty is transient and will 'like a neglected rose' wither if not enjoyed. These strategies are almost clichés and are abundant in Donne's 'The Flea' and 'The Ecstacy' and in Marvell's 'To His Coy Mistress'. But while Donne's and Marvell's listeners remain silent and, one assumes, enchanted, Milton allows The Lady to reply:

> *I had not thought to have unlocked my lips*
> *In this unhallowed air, but that this juggler*
> *Would think to charm my judgement, as mine eyes,*
> *Obtruding false rules pranked in reason's garb.*

(755–8)

The closing line of this extract is remarkable: 'false rules pranked in reason's garb' is a succinct and unambiguous rejection of the tendency in the verse of the Metaphysicals for the use of figurative language as a means of undermining the customary perceptions of the listener. Indeed it anticipates Samuel Johnson's famous dismissal of this technique: 'their learning instructs and their subtlety surprises; but the reader commonly thinks his improvement dearly bought...' (Johnson 1779–81). The Lady continues,

> *Thou hast not the ear nor soul to apprehend*
> *The subtle notion, and high mystery*
> *That must be uttered to unfold the sage*
> *And serious doctrine of Virginity...*
> *Enjoy your dear wit and gay rhetoric*
> *That hath so well been taught her dazzling fence*
> *Thou art not fit to hear thyself convinced.*

(783–91)

There are very few women in Renaissance literature who use language with such confidence and authority as Milton's Lady. Portia in *The Merchant of Venice* and Isabella in *Measure for Measure* are clever and effective advocates for their respective causes but their status is undermined by the fact that the former is only listened to when disguised as a man and the latter, irrespective of her intellectual capacities, is a pawn in a male-dominated game.

The Brothers eventually arrive 'with swords drawn' and transport their sister from Comus's realm of debased enchantment, but The Lady has already effectively disempowered Comus by undermining his rhetoric. As he puts it, 'I feel that I do fear / Her words set off by some superior power' (799–800).

The exchange anticipates the one that would take place in Book IX of *Paradise Lost*, between Satan and Eve, with one obvious difference: Eve, despite her precocity, is persuaded and precipitates the Fall of mankind.

It is evident that Milton, even when creating a night of enter-tainment, was aware of another duty as a poetic authority, someone who would cause his audience in the midst of their enjoyment to stop and think. He had not, while still in his early twenties, attempted to claim for himself the role of the modern epic poet, but thirty years later he would.

In 1637 he wrote to his friend Charles Diodati that he had become particularly concerned with history. He knew well the Greek and Roman theorists of philosophy and politics, but he was equally intrigued by the ways in which classical maxims of government had been variously cited and disintegrated by the warring factions of Europe through the dark ages and during the later medieval period. He had begun to feel that the so-called purer times of early Christianity were to some extent a myth, and was becoming more convinced that the real opportunity for Christian contentment and equilibrium was more recent. He summarized church history as 'after many a tedious age, the long deferred but much more wonderful and happy reformation... in these latters day' (WJM, III, p. 326). This was his only comment during this period on the religious controversies that had beset Europe for a century and his implication that the 'Reformation' might now have reached its culmination might well have been prompted by a sense that in England the true reformers were entering a desperate decisive struggle for survival.

William Laud's forces of conservative Anglo-Catholicism had, by 1637, gained complete control of the church and had begun to make use of ecclesiastic courts to supplant the instruments of secular power. Puritan clerics and preachers – all now effectively forbidden from taking up or remaining in posts – were being persecuted as common citizens and censored as speakers and writers. John Bastwick and Henry Burton had like William Prynne produced numerous pamphlets which advertised Puritan theology and religious practice, and accused the Laudian estab-lishment and royal family of courting Catholicism under the disguise of Anglicanism. All three were arrested and summoned before ecclesiastical courts, bodies which refused the accused the protection of Common Law. Each received the same sentence and in June 1637 they were flogged publicly in London and their ears were then hacked off.

In 1635 Milton's father had moved from Hammersmith to a grander house in the village of Horton a few miles further west. The village, adjacent to the royal palace of Windsor, was idyllically rural, its main houses circling a green and at its centre a pretty church of Norman vintage. On the outskirts was the medieval manor house of Henry Bulstrade, the principal land-owner in the locality. Milton senior rented from Bulstrade the second most prestigious house of the area, Berkin Manor, which stood in its own spacious grounds to the east of the village. The original building was demolished in the mid-nineteenth century and replaced by a large farmhouse in the Elizabethan red-brick style which carries the same name. Milton had stayed with the family and continued with his regime of private study, but in 1636–7 the equilibrium of his detached existence would be unsettled. His father, five years retired, was visited by summonses and law suits relating to share dealings with clients of a decade earlier. These would be settled but they reminded his son that the world was something that one was obliged to experience as well as observe.

On 3rd April 1637 his mother died, an event which brought the family together and united them in a sense of loss. The year, to Milton, would have seemed characterised by endings and terminations. In January he had attended the funeral of the Countess of Derby, effectively his patroness. William Sound, one of his St Paul's teachers, died a month after that, and during August, London mourned the passing of a figure who seemed to many to be the last remaining representative of a literary generation: Ben Jonson was buried in Westminster Abbey on 6th August.

In the same month Milton heard of the death at sea of one of his near contemporaries from Cambridge, Edward King, who had, following graduation, been elected to a Fellowship at Christ's

College: King also was a poet. Whether Milton and King had been close friends or passing acquaintances would become a contentious point for the former's biographers because it was not so much King's short life and tragic death that has caused him to be remembered to this day but a poem by Milton on both called 'Lycidas'.

The piece was commissioned by John Alsop, a Fellow of Christ's, as part of the collection of commemorative verses entitled *Obsequies for Edward King, lost at sea...* The other twelve verses have largely been forgotten but 'Lycidas' became a literary event in its own right and is, after *Paradise Lost*, Milton's most complex, puzzling and intensely scrutinized poem. It is, ostensibly and as required, a memorial to King, but its real subject is its author. It has frequently been compared with a piece of music, not because it was intended for song but as a consequence of its curious and unpredictable shifts in tone, subject and perspective. Some found this to be an anticipation of changing harmonies of the symphony (Nicholson, p. 105), but in truth it bears a closer resemblance to the radical, modernist literary technique of constantly altering the style and the perceived speaking presence of the text. King's death is its starting point but thereafter it takes us through reflections on the nature of poetry, the complexities of religious belief, and political and theological conflict, all of which are interwoven with intimations of something terrible and apocalyptic about to happen. Why Milton produced such a strange piece of work can best be addressed by treating it as an allegory. While Milton's memorial to King is sincere enough it also serves as a pretext for exploring the world from which the latter had recently departed.

In the middle of the poem Milton takes us to the banks of the 'Camus' (103), the Latin name for the Cam. Earlier in the piece Cambridge had been introduced as the intellectual home of King and Milton, but this time we return there to address a religious and political agenda. Suddenly we are introduced to 'the pilot of the Galilean lake' (109) who bears 'Two massy keys... of metal twain'. This is an allusion to St Peter, to whom Christ gave the symbolic keys of the true Church; it was the central divisive issue of the Reformation. The Papacy was regarded by Roman Catholics as the legacy of St Peter, its authority licensed by Christ, while many Protestants treated Rome as the corrupt usurper of Christ's word. Cambridge, as we have seen, had by this time become a microcosm of this dispute and the Anglo-Catholics who by 1637 gained control of the city, and of the Church of England, are introduced as the 'Blind mouths'. John Ruskin (*Sesame and Lilies*, I, p. 22) has offered the most enduring explanation of this image: 'A "Bishop" means "a person who sees". A "Pastor" means "a person who feeds"' he argued, and concluded that 'Blind mouths' refers to the higher clergy of the Laudian church who deserved neither the title of bishop, since they had blinded themselves to Christian truth, nor the generic term pastor since they were greedy and corrupt. They:

> *Scarce themselves know how to hold*
> *A sheep-hook, or have learned aught else the least*
> *That the faithful herdsman's art belongs*

> (119–20)

They are not the shepherd pastors who would care for their flock, but hedonists more concerned with the 'lean and flashy songs' of high ceremony. 'The hungry sheep' (125) have already become prey to 'the grim wolf with privy paw' (125) – the Roman Catholic Church – who 'Daily devours apace, and nothing said' (129). But Milton warns that the

> *two handed-engine at the door,*
> *Stands ready to smite once, and smite no more.*

> (130–1)

The general consensus is that this instrument is the broad-sword or axe that will be wielded by Protestantism against the

Anglo-Catholic hierarchy, a shrewd diagnosis of the tensions that within five years would lead to civil war.

Aside from the poems and the brief enigmatic letters, all that remain from Milton's reclusive period are his Commonplace Books in which he made notes on the vast range of material he scrutinized. These amounted to an index in prose, a sequence of comments by Milton on all he had read, listed according to his own subject-classifications. Under 'Ethical' are specified the sub-categories of 'moral evil', 'avarice', 'gluttony', 'suicide', 'curiosity', 'music', 'sloth', 'lying' and 'knowledge of literature'. It is intriguing that he associates literature and music, if only by implication, with issues that are by their nature fundamental and all-encompassing. By comparison, matters 'Economic' involve 'food', 'conduct', 'matrimony', 'the education of children', 'poverty', 'alms' and 'usury', and in the 'Political' section we encounter 'state', 'kings', 'subjects', 'nobility', 'property and taxes', 'plague', 'athletic games' and 'public shows'. Notably, the pragmatics and diversions of existence ('poverty', 'kings', 'subjects', 'matrimony', 'athletic games', 'public shows') belong in separate – and dare one say, lesser? – categories while 'knowledge of literature' is part of the field of ethics. This is quite a radical perception of what literature – and in this regard literature involved almost exclusively poetry – meant. Even its more enthusiastic champions during the Renaissance conceded that verse was an entertaining subsidiary to such serious discourses as philosophy and theology.

The Commonplace Books are prescient in that many of the entries anticipate some of his most controversial treatises of the Cromwellian years. He makes copious notes on Tertullian's and Cyprian's observations on public shows and popular entertainment without comment, but their relevance is self-evident: this was the period in which Calvinists and High Church clerics seemed obsessively preoccupied with the morality, or otherwise, of entertainment. He is more outspoken on his defence of marriage both for ordinary clergy and bishops and goes so far as to argue that polygamy among some Jewish sects should be tolerated. The Civil War had not yet begun but here is his view on the status of the 'King': 'The name of kings has always been hateful to free peoples, and he [God] condemns the action of the Hebrews in choosing to exchange their freedom for servitude' (*CPW*, I, p. 440).

He was forming opinions, based on a regime of evaluative research, but for what purpose? He did not even hint at what his particular ambition or vocation might be. But, in the manner of closing a circle, let us consider his apparent elevation of poetry to a state of intellectual significance in relation to his unortho-dox comments on the church, marriage, kingship et al and then look at his reflections on Dante's notions of choice and fate: 'The nature of each person should be especially observed and not bent in another direction; for God does not intend all people for one thing, but each one for his own work' (*CPW*, I, p. 405). This is, admittedly, enigmatic but with hindsight it is possible to inter-pret it as an attempt by Milton to reconcile his undoubted talent, as a poet, with his deeply felt religious, political and social opin-ions. How might he harness the latter to the former? Political poets were, at the time, an unknown quantity. Later, however, apocalyptic events would force Milton's affiliations together.

He had become aware that his programme of self-absorbed reading and study must soon end (see 'Letter to a Friend', *CPW,* I, p. 319), but he was not certain of what would follow it. Briefly, he took rooms at the Inns of Court, presumably with thoughts of following his brother into the legal profession; but he stayed there only for a few weeks. It is likely that his studies of the history of the civilised world had reached a natural conclusion. He now confronted the present day and what he saw caused him to think again about his role, his duty. As a poet, in 'Lycidas', he presented the reader with a vision of uncertainty, possibly catas-trophe. The tensions between the London-based Anglo-Catholic hierarchy and their pro-Calvinist counterparts in Scotland had moved beyond theological debate and would, in 1639, spill over into military conflicts – brief and inconclusive but anticipatory of the Civil War.

What did Milton do? He chose to go abroad, to Europe. This decision might appear symptomatic of at best self possession and at worst indifference, but it was quite the opposite. The intellectual, political, religious divisions of England had their origins further south: Calvinism, Catholicism, the Renaissance fabric of intellectual and aesthetic radicalism, were the products of Continental Europe. Milton, in order to become fully aware of what he could contribute to the condition of his homeland, first needed to encounter its influences.

Europe

Milton went first to France, then to Italy and finally to Geneva before returning to London in 1639. His locations were cautiously selected in that, in late 1637, he corresponded with Sir Henry Wotton, retired diplomat and then Provost of Eton College, on where and how he might encounter the best embodiments of European culture and religious doctrine (see Wilson, pp. 70–1). He was fluent in French and Italian, and his Latin – still the principal language of cultural exchange – was flawless.

In May 1638 he sailed, with one servant, for France and soon after spent time in Paris where he met Hugo Grotius, Dutchman, diplomat, poet and theologian, who was at the time promoting an alliance of states, principally England, Denmark, Holland and Sweden, which would form itself into a Pan-Protestant league. Nothing came of Grotius's scheme and nothing is known of Milton's views on it. His stay in Paris was brief, no more than five days, and according to Cyriack Skinner he had 'no admiration' for the kingdom's 'manners and Genius', (Darbishire, p. 19) a rather cryptic observation which might be taken to reflect Milton's probable opinions on the authoritarian Catholic regime of Louis XIII and Cardinal Richelieu, the latter having become legendary in his persecution of Huguenots. Later in *Of Education* (1644) Milton commented that educational reform in England would spare the moneyed classes the once fashionable habit of sending their young to 'the *Mounsieurs of Paris* [who] take our hopefull youth into their slight and prodigall custodies and send them over back again transform'd into mimics, apes and kicshoes' (*CPW*, II, p. 414). He was not so much deriding the competence of French educators as rebuking their culture of inflexible religious doctrine.

After Paris he went south to Nice and this would have been the most taxing part of his expedition. Rural France of the early seventeenth century had changed little since the middle ages. The only individuals who regularly travelled great distances were members of the gentry and aristocracy who were either accompanied by a small army of servants or found hospitality in the chateaux of their peers. Carriages for the ordinary traveller and inns providing meals and overnight accommodation were almost non-existent. It is likely that Milton and his servant traversed almost the whole of France on horseback and between substantial towns they would often have slept and prepared food in the open air.

From Nice they took a boat to Genoa. It should be pointed out that, at this time, Italy as a single political entity did not exist. It was a region made up of principalities and city-states, most, to varying degrees, influenced and controlled by Spain.

For Milton it involved refractions and exaggerations of his life in England. He had already become something of a polymath, an archetypal Renaissance man, and now he found himself in the crucible of the Renaissance. In Rome, Naples and Florence he attended concerts, viewed private collections of pictures and sculpture and marvelled at the assembly of gothic, neo-classical and baroque styles that made these cities in themselves works of art. At Naples he stayed with Giovanni Manso, who kept a villa just outside the city. Arguably the most eminent Italian poet of the age, Manso had known Tasso and Marini, Italy's finest sixteenth-century writers whose English equivalents would have been, respectively, Spenser and Donne. More significantly Manso, Tasso and Marini were part of a lineage which originated in the fourteenth century with Petrarch. They were the embodiments and inheritors of the essential Renaissance. (Before his visit to Italy Milton had become intimately familiar with the works of Dante Aligheri (1265–1321) whose *Divine Comedy* was the only major Christian epic prior to *Paradise Lost*.)

Surprisingly, given Milton's age and slightness of works in print, his own reputation went before him. He was received in the houses of the nobility and in private academies as a figure of coming greatness. During March 1639, for example, he was invited on two occasions to give readings of his Latin and English poems in the celebrated Svogliati Academy in Florence.

Italy projected him into an idyll of cosmopolitan art and at the same time offered him a perverse vision of religious authoritarianism. Practically all of his hosts were Catholics – he even stayed for a while in the Palace of Cardinal Berberini, the Pope's nephew – and in general it seemed that a shared reverence for European culture transcended religious difference – Milton's Protestant views were as well known as his poetry. Yet within this atmosphere of intellectual and aesthetic exuberance he found also an atmosphere of repression. The Traveller's Book of the English Jesuit College in Rome records that on 30th October 1638 'Mr John Milton, with his servant' along with three other named English visitors dined in the College 'and were magnificently received'. There are no accounts of the exchanges of that evening but other evidence indicates that Milton during his stay in the city caused some controversy. He stayed with Manso after leaving Rome and intended to return to the Papal State following a brief excursion to Sicily. He was, however, advised by his host to change his plans and to depart from Italy for his own safety. He later reported that he was also 'warned by merchants that they had learned through letters of plots laid against me by the English Jesuits, should I return to Rome, because of the freedom with which I had spoken about religion' (*CPW*, IV., p. 619).

Manso was not reprimanding him; quite the contrary. He was advising Milton that his continued presence would be dangerous for both of them. One might suspect that Milton was representing himself with benefit of imaginative licence as a hero abroad, brave defender of the true faith in the heartland of Catholicism. A more objective witness, Nicolaas Heinsius, who had known some of the priests who were in Rome during Milton's visit, wrote in 1653, 'That Englishman [Milton] was hated by the Italians, among whom he lived a long time... because he both disputed freely about religion, and on any occasion whatever prated very bitterly against the Roman Pontiff' (French, III, p. 322). Yet he returned to Rome. 'What I was, if any man inquired, I concealed from no-one. For almost two months, in the very stronghold of the Pope, if anyone attacked the orthodox religion [Protestantism], I openly, as before, defended it. Thus, by the will of God, I returned again in safety to Florence' (*CPW,* IVI.1, p. 619).

Here he was particularly distressed by his meeting with a legendary presence, the astronomer Galileo, who by Papal decree had effectively become a prisoner in his own villa close to the city. Galileo, the disinterested empiricist, had observed the universe and reported facts which went against religious orthodoxy. Six years later during the English Civil War, Milton, in *Areopagitica,* recalled the meeting with Galileo, 'grown old a prisoner to the Inquisition, for thinking otherwise than the Franciscan and Dominican licensers thought'. This might seem a predictably anti-Catholic comment but elsewhere in the same document Milton notes, with retrospective irony, that his Italian acquaintances had frequently expressed an admiration for England as the paragon of multi-denominational tolerance and free speech. He knew better.

It is more than likely that Milton's period abroad served to complicate – sometimes undermine, often refresh – his views of the Continent acquired during his years of retirement and research outside London. Some of the figures and institutions he encountered, particularly Catholics, reinforced the stereotypes of the Puritan pamphlets but more often he came across a spectrum of unpredictabilities where indulgence and free thinking predominated. He wrote later:

I could recount what I have seen and heard in other Countries, where this kind of inquisition tyrannizes; when I have sat among their lerned men, for that honour I had, and bin counted happy to be born in such a place of *Philosophic* freedom, as they suppos'd England was, while themselvs did nothing but bemoan the servil condition into which lerning amongst them was brought; that this was it which had dampt the glory of Italian wits; that nothing had bin there writt'n now these many years but Flattery and fustian. There it was that I found and visited the famous *Galileo* grown old, a prisner to the Inquisition... And though I knew that England then was groaning loudest under the Prelaticall yoak, never-thelesse I took it as a pledge of future happines, that other Nations were so perswaded of her liberty... (*CPW*, II, pp. 537–8)

Florence had impressed him most, yet despite enjoying the hospitality and erudition of many there he was aware that ex-changes on such fundamental issues as religious belief were a dangerous undertaking. 'I would not indeed begin a conversation about religion, but if questioned about my faith would hide nothing, whatever the consequences' (*CPW*, II, p. 794). He never had to endure the 'consequences' but he was aware that such a licence to relative free speech was granted to him *because* he was a foreigner. Citizens of what were once the pioneering states of the Renaissance could now only 'bemoan' their 'servil condition' and do so largely in private.

Before leaving Italy, Milton visited Venice, the most tolerant state of the region, probably of Europe. It maintained lay juris-diction over the Inquisition and the censors, and continued to forbid entry to all Jesuits, until 1657. It even supported the sover-eignty of the Protestant Grisons, in neighbouring Valtellina, against attempted Spanish incursions. Milton made no reference to his impressions of the city state but one wonders if its admir-able yet precipitous condition inspired the passage in *Areopagitica* in which he expresses hope for the future of England, despite unpropitious circumstances: 'I took it as a pledge of future happines, that other Nations were so persuaded of her liberty'.

He went from Italy to Geneva, from the home of Catholicism to the hub of radical Protestantism; there he spent time with Giovanni Diodati, an eminent Calvinist theologian and uncle of his friend Charles. Milton was with Giovanni when he was informed by letter from England of Charles's untimely death, though some believe that he first heard of it by word of mouth when staying with Manso in Naples. Parts of London in 1638–9 were stricken by the plague and Diodati was thought to have contracted the disease. He had been Milton's closest friend and most intimate confidant and it is possible that his sense of tragic loss coalesced, however obliquely, with his other perceptions of what was unfolding in England. It is certain that while in Italy he had been informed of the so-called Bishops' War, an inconclusive conflict which had arisen out of Charles I and Laud's attempts to force the Scots to accept Episcopal liturgy. In Geneva he learnt of a related but potentially more devastating conflict that was brewing between the king and Parliament. Before 1639 Milton would have perceived for himself a multiplicity of destinies, as poet, philosopher, and commentator upon his age. Suddenly he found that these honourable but somewhat unfocused commitments were becoming specified. His country would soon be at war with itself. He went home.

The Civil War and
Early Political Writing

The English Civil War was never officially declared by either side; understandably, given that both thought themselves to be the true representatives of the same nation. The first major, and indecisive, battle between the Royalist and Parliamentarian forces was fought at Edgehill in south Warwickshire in October 1642, but a conflict in various forms had been taking place for more than two years before that. The Scots had established a National Covenant in 1638, which was a religious assembly committed to the resistance of Charles and Laud's doctrine and policies but bore a disturbing resemblance to an alternative seat of government. The consequent skirmishes between Scots and Royalist detachments were inconclusive but Charles was set upon the defeat of the rebellious northerners and in 1639 called an English Parliament to raise money for a second onslaught. The Commons refused and when in November 1640 he tried again they went further and embarked upon a policy of active resistance. They tried and executed his first minister the Earl of Strafford and Archbishop Laud was arrested and sent to the Tower, where he would remain until his execution in 1645.

The imprisoned Puritan critics of the Royalist government were released, the king was compelled to abolish the Prerogative Courts, through which he had persecuted dissenters, and was obliged to accept a Bill which perpetuated the present Parliament until such time as it chose to dissolve itself. Finally, when asked to relinquish his control of the permanent army to Parliament, he refused and with his private guard attempted to take physical control of Parliament and arrest its most prominent arbiters as they sat in session. He failed, riots ensued and the king fled from London in 1641 to Oxford, which for the next five years would become the Royalist capital and headquarters for military operations.

This was the London to which Milton had returned in 1639, and it was a disturbing place. Families were becoming divided; old friends, colleagues and neighbours were separated by choice and affiliation. By 1641–2 many supporters of the Royalist cause had left the city; it seemed like a besieged encampment. Milton would have witnessed the mixture of terror and resolve which beset the city when Charles, after Edgehill, in November 1642, tried and almost succeeded in retaking it from the Parliamentarians.

These events are addressed in Milton's Sonnet VII. He was living in Aldersgate Street and the poem is addressed to

> *Captain or colonel, or knight in arms,*
> *Whose chance on these defenceless doors may seize,*
>
> (1–2)

and is largely a plea for mercy by 'him within': Milton. It cites the sacking of Thebes by Alexander the Great (referred to as the 'Emathian conqueror') after which the house and descendants of Pindar were spared, and paraphrases a passage from Plutarch which describes how, after the Spartans had taken Athens, a song from Euripides' *Electra* had prevented them from razing a city that had produced so great a poet.

It is a peculiar piece because, superficially, it seems to involve on Milton's part abject surrender and a rather selfish request for compassion. Lines 5–6, paraphrased, state that 'I John Milton, poet, will repay your mercy with words of praise'.

He can requite thee, for he knows the charms
That call fame on such gentle acts as these

(5–6)

However, it is generally assumed that the sonnet's candid evocation of fear and desperation on the poet's part is an act of solidarity with his fellow citizens of London, a realistic and personal register of the feeling of terror and panic that gripped the city at the prospect of its largely Parliament-affiliated inhabitants being massacred by their vengeful Royalist captors.

He would see the results of the successful defence, as suspected Royalist conspirators were hanged before the doors of their own houses. Some of them he would have known. He knew certainly that his own brother, Christopher, then in Reading, was a supporter of the Royalist cause.

Witness to all of this he most certainly was, but not participant. In 1639, deciding not to return to his father's rural home in Horton, he had set up in Aldersgate Street a private academy for the young sons of the aspiring middle classes (Edward Phillips, his nephew and eventually his first biographer, was one of his pupils). Samuel Johnson, from the safe distance of more than a century, pours mockery upon a 'man who hastens home because his countrymen are contending for their liberty, and when he reaches the scene of the action, vapours away his patriotism in a private boarding school'. Johnson's contempt for Milton as a man and a poet is unswerving, and he ignores evidence, supplied by Phillips and others, that the academy enabled Milton to prepare himself as a participant in the turmoil to come.

The enterprise might have been inspired by his experience of the similar university-style institutions run by the intellectuals of Florence, but its purpose was more pragmatic. He still received income from his father's investments, but he wanted a degree of independence and a base in London. From here, particularly during the decade of the 1640s when the Civil War was tearing the country apart, he shifted his affiliation away from poetry and toward political-theological thinking.

A record of his thoughts on this can be found in the Trinity Manuscript, which contains rough notes from the period between 1639 and early 1641 in which he explored ideas for a major piece of writing. This would probably take the form of 'A Heroicall Poem', and he considers a narrative on the emergence of England as a sovereign state, involving episodes from the Roman Conquest, 'Alfred's reigne, especially at his issuing out of Edelingsay on the Danes, whose actions are wel like those of Ulysses' (*TM*, p. 38), and the Norman invasion and its consequences. Clearly he was interested in researching the permutations of a long history, which might cast light on the state of a nation now on the brink of crisis. The list carries the heading 'British Trag[eddies]'. His other hypothesis incorporates themes from the Old and New Testaments. Some involve Abraham, 'or Isaak redeemd' but most are concerned with Genesis and the Fall, the origin of the human condition.

Clearly he was oscillating between two ways of explaining the forthcoming war, a conflict that would tear his homeland apart. Should he go to the Bible, seek the wisdom of the apostles and prophets on what human beings could be and do? Or should he address those questions in what we now term a rational, humanist manner, consulting history for solutions? He chose the latter, and abandoned the 'Heroicall Poem' as his vehicle: he would become a pamphleteer. Much later, after the Civil War, he would return to poetry and to the Old Testament, but when he did so his true subject matter was still the horrific nature of more recent events.

The pamphlet, a short treatise published separately and usually without hard covers, had risen to prominence during the later part of the Elizabethan period. In the 1590s a series of anonymous pamphlets published under the pen name of Martin Marprelate caused enormous controversy by publicly urging the government to purge the church of its corrupt bishops and establish a Presbyterian structure. The authorities were so alarmed that they commissioned writers such as Thomas Nashe and John Lyly to reply on their behalf. Pamphleteering was effectively the beginning of journalism; opinionated free speech in print. Elizabeth's government recognised its dangerous potential and imposed severe restrictions on the press. These became even more stringent during the reign of Charles I but, after the departure of the king from London, pamphleteering was reborn as the public forum for practically every controversy of immediate relevance; politics and religion being the core issues. Milton became one of the most prolific pamphleteers of the age. Generally he supported the Parliamentarian cause but he was by no means its uncritical apologist. His pamphlets of the 1640s are marked by their projection of unsettled contemporary issues into the practical sphere of the manner in which the country would be governed after the war and its results, the implied assumption being that the Parliamentarians would be the victors.

One of the first, *Of Reformation. Touching Church Discipline* (1641), addresses itself to the major issues that had divided the Church of England between the High Church and the opposing Puritan/Presbyterian factions, particularly the existence and status of bishops within the church hierarchy – and on this Milton sided with the Puritans. More significantly, the pamphlet offers, in the manner of a modern feature article on contemporary politics, a survey of the state of the Reformation. In Milton's view Protestantism had become an ineffectual shadow of its earlier, inspired manifestation, so fraught with division that it now lacked direction or purpose. He does not specify a solution but rather implies that once the present conflict is settled (like many others he took the optimistic view that the war would be over within a year) reason will prevail and church will cooperate with government in a purposive relationship. The mood of *Of Reformation* drifts between the impertinent, the speculative and the naive. Its title indicates its central hypothesis, the idealised vision of England after the Civil War which he foresees as populated by individuals like himself, willing and able to stand outside organised religion and government: 'tis not the common law nor the civil, but piety and justice that are our foundresses; they stoop not, neither change colour, for Aristocracy, Democracy or Monarchy' (*WJM*, III, p. 69). This thesis sums up the somewhat unfocused idealism of the Parliamentarian Independents: guaranteed freedom of religious thought will in itself ensure some kind of civic idyll; personal morality, based mainly but not strictly on the Bible, will supplant the factionalism and corruption of previous relations between church, government and the individual. When we compare this with his later prose writings, when he moved closer to the victorious Cromwellian ascendancy, we find that pragmatism usurped idealism, not completely but sufficiently to suggest that, for Milton, the Civil War was a horribly educative process. Here we should look forward to *Paradise Lost*. Milton in the early years of the Civil War perceived the conflict as precipitate to the best that could be hoped for by fallen man. The consequences of the Fall would not be rescinded but human beings could organise themselves in a way that both accommodated and improved upon the future shown to Adam by the angel Michael. When it is shown to him in Books XI and XII of *Paradise Lost* the optimism is far more subdued: by then Milton himself had witnessed the dismantling of the Parliamentarian ideal.

In *The Reason of Church Government,* published a year later in 1642, he continues with the same theme, but there is a striking section in the second book in which the subject becomes himself, his past, his family, his beliefs and his reputation throughout the continent as a poet. It reads sometimes like a piece of egotistical self-promotion, but its true purpose, albeit more implied than clearly stated, was to enable him to reflect upon his work so far as a rehearsal for a greater task. What exactly this would be is implied also. For the reader of the pamphlet it might appear that he is introducing himself as an authority, a spokesman, commentator and promulgator of ideas that would inform the governance and condition of the new England. (One should note that his first three pamphlets were anonymous while this, his fourth, was published under his own name.) Perhaps presenting himself as a poet with a duty carried a private resonance because among Milton's manuscript papers would later be discovered plans and early drafts for a dramatic poem, provisionally entitled *Adam Unparadized*, on which he was working during the time of the pamphlets. This would explain the Fall and the subsequent condition of mankind, and it was of course the prototype for *Paradise Lost*.

The Reason of Church Government is a curious document. Certainly within it Milton celebrates his own status as a poet, but he also rationalises, contextualises this role.

> For although a poet soaring in the high region of his fancies with his garland and singing robes about him might without apology speak more of himself than I mean to do, yet for me sitting here in the cool element of prose…

He is contrasting the imaginative, unworldly realm of verse with the 'cool' specifics of prose, and initiating himself as a prose writer, someone who will engage with the practicalities of life. He does so and he imagines the England that will emerge from the ongoing conflict,

> because the spirit of man cannot demean itself lively in this body without some creating intermission of labour and serious things, it were happy for the commonwealth if our magistrates, as in those famous governments of old, would take into their care… the managing of our public sports and festival pastimes, that they might be… such as may inure and harden our bodies by martial exercises to all warlike skill and performance, and may civilise, adorn, and make discreet our minds by the learned and affable

meeting of frequent academics, and the procurement of wise and artful recitations sweetened with eloquent and graceful enticements to the love and practice of justice, temperance, and fortitude, instructing and bettering the notion at all opportunities... Whether this may not be, not only in pulpits, but after other persuasive method, at set and solemn panegyrize, in theatres, porches, or what other place or way may win most upon the people to receive at once both recreation and instruction, let them in authority consult. (*WJM*, III, pp. 239–40)

This vision was partly inspired by his visit to Florence but in a broader sense he is imagining England as a Christian, Protestant recreation of the Athenian and Roman states: worship, labour, sport, the intellect, the conditions of daily life will be incorporated and attuned. Again we should compare this with his prose writings of the late 1640s, when he had become an active member of the new republic, and note that the speculative idyll is replaced by conditional pragmatism.

The pamphlets introduced Milton to a new discourse. He had at Cambridge refined his skills as a rhetorician and now he was adapting these largely oral exercises to print and prose. He could be a combative and uncharitably polemical writer. For example, in *Of Reformation* he employs vividly repulsive imagery, emphasizing the morbid excesses of the human condition, in his attacks upon the prelates. Those raised to a bishopric 'exhale and reake out' the previously commendable zeal, producing 'a queasy temper of luke-warmnesse that gives a Vomit to God himselfe' (*CPW*, I, pp. 536–7). Bishops infect the body of the church with 'an universall rottenness and gangrene' and those appointed by Laud spend their tenure 'belching the soure Crudities of yesterdays *Paperie*' (p. 540). He suffered fools – that is opponents – ungladly and his acerbic, aggressive tendencies become harshly evident in his *Animadversions upon a Remonstrant's Defence against Smectymnuus* (1641). 'Smectymnuus' as everyone knew was an assembly of the initials of five Presbyterian clergymen who were involved in an ongoing public debate by pamphlet with Bishop Joseph Hall, a Laudian divine, on Protestant theology and ecclesiastical practice. (One of the former was Thomas Young, 'TY', Milton's childhood tutor with whom he had remained in contact.) Irrespective of the theological content of *Animadversions* what is most striking is its author's ability to blend scholastic authority with bombast and ridicule.

One of his most intriguing pamphlets is *Of Education* (1644). It is radical, revolutionary, in its formulation of an education system which would unite the country and bring together all of its citizens within a fabric of learning, a collective sense of identity and duty. Matthew Arnold was to suggest something similar in the mid-nineteenth century and the 1945 Labour government attempted to implement a socialist version, but Milton pre-empted both. The pamphlet is influenced by Milton's experiences in St Paul's, Cambridge and Italy. He suggests that all citizens (aged between twelve and twenty-one) should be instructed not only in the classics but in contemporary literature and thought (no doubt recalling Gill at St Paul's) and that a network of institutions should be set up throughout the nation which would combine the perceived roles of school and university. Instruction and freethinking would productively interact. 'The end then of learning is to repair the ruins of our first parents by possessing our souls of true vertue' (*CPW*, II, p. 367). The breadth of ambition encompassed in this brief statement of purpose is extraordinary. He goes so far as to claim that the opportunities promised by the unprecedented post-war nation will enable men to strive for a degree of understanding denied to us after the Fall of Adam and Eve. Two decades later Milton invites the reader of Book XII of *Paradise Lost* to compare the vision of *Of Education* with the weary resignation of Adam, who has just been advised by the angel Michael on the severe limits of his intellectual aspirations.

Greatly instructed I shall hence depart
Greatly in peace of thought, and have my fill
Of knowledge.

(537–9)

Adam, after the Fall, knows he must curb his ambitions and his author, Milton, following the fall of the Cromwellian republic, is aware that his hopes for what that environment might have inspired will now come to nothing.

Milton's 1644 curriculum for his new academies is, even by today's standards, outstandingly original. In their early teens pupils would combine the study of core classical subjects – including Latin and Greek grammar, the major texts of both classical traditions – with modern languages, particularly Italian, German, French and Spanish – each of which would enable the pupil to communicate directly with hostile and friendly nations in Europe. Moral philosophy derived from the work of Plato, Xenophon, Cicero, Plutarch et al would be taught alongside scripture. Literature – ancient and modern – would be accorded an equal status to philosophy. A similarly revolutionary regime would extend beyond the arts and humanities, with arithmetic, geometry, zoology, anatomy, agriculture and geography combined with such pragmatic skills as architecture, military engineering, medicine, economics and fortification. Erudite classicists – the equivalents of schoolmasters and university dons – would as teachers hold the same status as 'Hunters, fowlers, Fishermen, Shepherds, Gardeners, *Apothecaries*... Architects... Engineers, Mariners, *Anatomists*' (*CPW*, II, pp. 393–4). This systematic clearance of barriers between high academic learning and the pragmatics of the national infrastructure – including business, defence, trade and politics – is genuinely revolutionary. It is based upon the premise, the idyll, of a nation beyond internal division, united and at peace with itself. Unfortunately the so-called Commonwealth would involve nothing like this.

Milton's most debated and celebrated pamphlet is the *Areopagitica* (1644). It was prompted partly by an ordinance passed by the Commons in June of the same year by which the immense output of the London presses would thereafter be monitored and regulated by Parliament. By this time the Commons was dominated by an inbuilt majority of hardcore Presbyterians who were becoming unsettled by opinions, publicly voiced, and radical factions which had spun out of what was effectively a prototype republic. The Independents were arguing for the establishment of a constitution which licensed freedom of expression and religious commitment. They were themselves Protestants but they envisaged a post-war state in which no specific school of belief would dominate the secular organs of government. The Parliamentary ordinance was a reaction by the Presbyterians against the growing popularity of the Independents, whose spokesmen were making use of pamphlets to promote their ideas. It was as though the repressive dictatorship of Charles had been inherited by the Presbyterians who similarly feared anything that might threaten their autocratic pre-eminence. Milton, while remaining committed to the Cromwellian cause, was unsettled by the image of a post-war nation that was an authoritarian, Presbyterian, version of its High Church predecessor, and *Areopagitica* is an argument for religious freedom and free speech. He addresses the Parliament of England as if it were the democratic assembly of ancient Athenians assembled on the Areopagus (hence the title). *Areopagitica* promotes a condition of liberty and freedom of choice that would not properly feature in the socio-political mainstream of British life until the nineteenth century. It would, long after Milton's time, be plundered by those who wished to underpin their own libertarian ideas with quotations from what is often regarded as the first systematic defence of free speech. Consider, for example, the following assault upon the practice of censorship.

As good kill a man as kill a good book; who kills a man kills
a reasonable creature, Gods image; but he who destroys a
good book, kills reason itself, kills the image of God, as it
were, in the eye. (*WJM*, IV, pp. 297–8)

Milton's presentation of himself in *The Reason of Church
Government* as a poet with the wisdom and authority of a
philosopher is here fully justified. The passage deploys figurative
devices not as decoration but as constituents of a powerful, logically argued thesis, and it typifies the manner and technique of
the rest of the pamphlet.

Milton was aware that *Areopagitica* was a provocative and, for
him, potentially dangerous piece of work; arrest and imprisonment seemed distinct possibilities. In fact, Parliament responded
in an unexpected and quite effective manner; they ignored it.
They did not ever discuss the repeal of the printing ordinance.
Six months after it was published, Prynne, a fully established
polemicist and supporter of Presbyterianism, published a
Parliament-sponsored pamphlet called *Fresh Discovery* in which
he assailed critics of the licensing laws. Milton was not mentioned, and one wonders if it had become an official government policy to pretend that he did not exist; if so, this might
perhaps be taken as a perverse compliment to his abilities.

Did Milton regard his treatment by the authorities as a personal slight? Perhaps, because little more than a year afterwards
he produced a short poem which reads like *Areopagitica* versified
and written by an angrier man. 'On the New Forces of
Conscience Under the Long Parliament' is a direct attack upon
the Presbyterians, whom he presents as an assembly of tyrants.
He actually names some of the, in his view, most authoritarian
and illiberal figures, such as Dr Adam Stewart, Samuel
Rutherford (line 8), Thomas Edwards and the 'Scotch What-
d'ye-call', thought to be Robert Bailie (line 12), all senior academics and theologians in Scotland and continental Europe. He
presents them as the new generation of theological dictators

and most significantly he compares them with the Roman Catholic hierarchy. Their influence upon Parliament is compared with the Council of Trent (14–15) in which the Catholic Church had reformulated its doctrines after the Reformation. He closes: 'New *Presbyter* is but old *Priest* writ large' (20). He does not suggest theological parallels between Catholicism and Presbyterianism; rather that both usurp civil and religious liberty and enforce doctrinaire belief as law. He contrasts the Presbyterians with

> *Men whose life, learning, faith and pure intent*
> *Would have been held in high esteem with Paul,*
>
> (TP: 8–9)

the Independents, with whom he sympathized; those who advocated civil liberty as the basis for a fabric of theological difference but who are 'now… named and printed heretics' (11). This line is thought to refer to the five authors of the tract called *Apologetical Narration* (1646), who sharply opposed the regulations of the Presbyterians and demanded toleration and freedom of conscience, and who, unlike Milton, would be made to answer to Parliament.

Milton had married Mary Powell in July 1642. He was thirty-three, she was seventeen. Their brief courtship and subsequent relationship have become the stuff of legend and imaginative speculation, the most sardonic example of the latter being Robert Graves's novel *Wife to Mr Milton* (1942). Some facts are known. Milton visited Oxford in June 1642 partly to examine documents in the Bodleian Library and partly, at the request of his father, to deal with some family business: a loan of £300 that Milton senior had some years before made to one Richard Powell of Forest Hill near Oxford and repayments of which had recently become infrequent. That these financial issues were eventually settled by all parties is generally assumed to be the case but what is more certain is that, as a guest of the Powells,

Milton met their eldest daughter, the pretty and engaging Mary, and within a month they were married.

The sequence of events has an air of romance about it in that during the summer of 1642 Oxford was already being treated as the base for the king and his military advisers, although Charles's presence there was not at the time permanent. Units of the Royalist and Parliamentarian armies were encamped at various points in the counties between Oxfordshire and London and within three months of Milton's visit one of the first major battles of the war would take place at Edgehill, twenty miles from Oxford, with more than 5,000 killed. The Powells, moreover, were ardent Royalists and what they thought of their unexpected visitor, already known to be the author of radical pro-Parliamentarian pamphlets, can only be imagined. However, Richard Powell agreed to the marriage and to a £1,000 dowry, money he did not really have.

Mary returned with her husband to Aldersgate Street in late July and if love at first sight had prompted their sudden union, the sensation would appear to have worn off with almost equal rapidity. It soon became evident to Milton that his bride, while beautiful and delicate in appearance, was in disposition and temperament his complete opposite. She had no interest in literature or contemporary ideas; her religion, High Church, was more an inheritance and habit than a fabric of beliefs.

After less than a month in London, Mary received a request from her father to return home to Oxford, which she did. No one knows why this request was made or what prompted the newly married woman to leave. At the time Royalists were leaving London in droves and perhaps her family feared for her safety. Edward Phillips, Milton's nephew, pupil and co-resident of Aldersgate Street, would have witnessed some of these events and in his biography of his uncle he tells how Milton assumed that her absence was temporary and was expecting her back for Michaelmas, 29th September. Indeed, Phillips's version is the only reasonably reliable source of information upon which later

writers have based their wild and sometimes fantastic speculations. He writes that Mary arrived at the house along with 'some
few of her nearest Relations' (Darbishire, p. 63). He does not say
who they were but apart from her parents, who did not accompany her to London, her 'nearest' would have been her twenty-
one-year-old brother Richard, her eighteen-year-old younger
brother, James, and her sister Anne, sixteen. Phillips suggests that
the likely cause of her swift departure was the fact that she had
suddenly found herself alone with a man whose regime of quiet-
ness and study was so unlike the lively environment of Forest
Hill. Bringing part of her family with her allowed her a period
of adjustment, in the sense that these siblings, close to her age,
would no doubt have imparted some of the Powell energy to the
subdued atmosphere of Aldersgate Street, but when they departed they took with them all that Mary had previously known.

> At length they took their leave, and returning to *Foresthill*,
> left the Sister behind; probably not much to her satisfaction,
> as appeared by the Sequel; but that time she had for a
> Month or thereabout led a Philosophical Life (after having
> been used to a great House, and much Company and
> Joviality). (Darbishire, p. 64)

Phillips goes on to describe how '*Michaelmas* being come,
and no news of his Wife's return, he sent for her by Letter; and
receiving no answer, sent several other Letters, which were also
unanswered.' Eventually, he resorted to a 'Foot-Messenger with
a Letter, desiring her return'; the messenger returned empty
handed and 'to the best of my remembrance, reported that
he was dismissed with some sort of Contempt' (p. 65). Phillips
gives the impression of being reluctant to apportion blame
where none is certain, and he suggests that Mary's apparent
snubbing of her new husband was due less to some caprice
of personality than the worsening of divisions within the nation.
He blames her family.

> This proceeding, in all probability, was grounded upon no
> other Cause but this, namely, that the Family being gener-
> ally addicted to the Cavalier Party, as they called it, and some
> of them possibly ingaged in the King's Service, who by this
> time had his Head Quarters at *Oxford*, and was in some
> Prospect of Success, they began to repent them of having
> Matched the Eldest Daughter of the Family to a Person so
> contrary to them in Opinion; and thought it would be a blot
> in their Escutcheon, when ever that Court should come to
> Flourish again. (Darbishire, p. 65)

They would not meet again until 1646, after the defeat of the King.

The connection between Mary's departure and the publication less than a year later by Milton of a pamphlet called *The Doctrine and Discipline of Divorce* (1643) seems so obvious as to be hardly worth comment, but the relationship between the event and the nature of the text is by no means straightforward. Critics have scoured the pamphlet for evidence of autobiographical inspiration and anger; there is little, if any. Mary's disappearance might have prompted the writing of it but the breadth and balanced complexity of the argument indicates clearly that Milton had been pondering and researching the topic long before he met his wife. The *Divorce* pamphlet was well planned and intended as another element of his programme of political and religious ideas.

Divorce had been legalized for entirely selfish reasons by Henry VIII – it was indeed a contributory factor in his break with Rome – but over the subsequent century it had rarely been made use of by anyone else. It involved complex, potentially humili-ating, and enormously expensive legal procedures. Milton's pamphlet was, as he made clear, designed as a cure for unhappi-ness, a proposal that couples who found themselves to be incom-patible should be given an easier opportunity to end their state of mutual distress. Existing canon law permitted divorce only in extreme circumstances, such as non-consummation or if either party were found to be planning the murder of the other, but

Milton argued that the distress caused by the enforced continuation of a relationship between 'two incoherent and uncombining dispositions' should, legally, be alleviated.

Parker states that 'It took almost fanatical courage that comes with overwhelming conviction in the face of accepted opinion, that kind of courage that will stand alone if it can stand on solid truth' (p. 242). He means that while Milton's reputation as a prose writer on politics and religion rivals that of Milton the poet, it should be remembered that in 1643 he was writing as an independent without the official protection or prompting of any of the parties and factions of a divided nation. He lived in a Cromwellian city and favoured the anti-Royalist cause but he was attacking enshrined canon law, and its advocates, the prelates, the bishops and hierarchy of the Anglican church, still held power within both camps. What exactly did he propose? His most controversial proposition was that marriage involved a meeting of minds, that the mutual sense of intellectual and temperamental compatibility was of far greater significance than such fundamental and provable issues as procreation or sexual betrayal. In his view a marriage which is comprised of 'two incoherent and uncombining dispositions' (*WJM*, III, p. 417) calls for its own dissolution. If this is denied the discontented party will find themselves 'bound fast to an uncomplying discord of nature', 'an image of earth and phlegm' (344–400), so much so that the result will be the worst imaginable: since marital love is a token of God's love for man its failure and absence will cause the believer even to sink from 'despair to thoughts of atheism' (405–6). There is a remarkable passage on adultery in which Milton takes it upon himself to overturn all standard interpretations of scripture which regard the act, by either party, as an unpardonable sin.

For that fault committed [adultery] argues not always a hatred either natural or incidental against whom it is committed; neither does it inferred a disability of all future

77

helpfulnes, or loyalty, or loving agreement, being once past, and pardon'd, where it can be pardon'd… a grave and prudent Law of *Moses*… contains a cause of divorce greater beyond compare then that for adultery… this being but a transient injury, and soon amended, I mean as to the party against whom the trespasse is.

(CPW, pp. 331–3)

However, before citing parallels between Milton's ideas and the liberal divorce legislation of the twentieth-first century one should note that in all instances he presents the man as the injured party. He does not deny that the woman also might suffer, but consistently she is portrayed as the potential cause of the state in which 'instead of being one flesh, they will be rather two carcasses chained unnaturally together' (p. 478). She is presented as such not because Milton regards women as more prone than men to such specifics as infidelity, but because more often than not it is the woman who has to prove her potential for social and intellectual compatibility. He gives an example: 'who knows that the bashful muteness of a virgin may oft times hide all the unliveliness and natural sloth which is really unfit for conversation? … nor is it therefore that for a modest error a man should forfeit so great a happiness – and no charitable means to release him' (p. 394). This might seem to us a somewhat patronising, almost misogynistic, representation of womanhood – the temptingly mute virgin might well prove to be genuinely stupid – but at the time it was radical, in that it is founded upon the assumption that a woman is at least capable of being the intellectual equal of a man.

Two points should be made about the significance of the divorce tract. First, its content reinforces the contention that it was not a perverse, personal diatribe. Mary evidently was not the model for the hypothetical wife who failed the test of intellectual compatibility: why else would he want her back and not sue for divorce? Second, the models for gender distinction and marriage presented in the tract prompt comparison with his treatment of the same issues in his poetry, particularly his presentation of The Lady in *Comus* and of course the original couple, Adam and Eve in *Paradise Lost*. In the former, the woman is the intellectual equal of her potential seducer, the obverse of the 'bashful muteness of a virgin'; virginity (pre-marital), for her, is part of an ethical fabric and not a tempting façade. She is, one must assume, the kind of woman who would be an active participant in Milton's idealised marriage of minds, while Comus the demon is the worst kind of man, unable to recognise the mental capacities of a woman. Adam and Eve are a more complex pairing. Divorce in the modern (i.e. post-Old Testament) sense is not an issue in *Paradise Lost* but in Book IX Adam faces a choice which is at least comparable with that of the injured party in a marriage. She has eaten the forbidden fruit. If he does likewise he will stay with his beloved, indeed his intellectual equal; if he does not he will obey God's law, but lose her. He eats. In the light of this moment in *Paradise Lost* consider Parker's summary of the divorce pamphlet.

> He [Milton] makes it quite clear that, in his opinion, divorce should not be permitted for malice, or for any 'accidental, temporary, or reconcilable offence' – not even for 'stubborn disobedience against the husband'. It should be permitted only for genuine and certain incompatibility, amply demonstrated. (p. 243)

The parallels between the divorce tract and the Book IX passage in *Paradise Lost* are striking, and unsettling. Eve's act does indeed involve 'stubborn disobedience against the husband', but does Adam's choice to follow her mean that he sees this as an 'accidental, temporary, or reconcilable offence'? It involves the breaking of God's law (the eating of the fruit), but so do 'malice' and for that matter adultery, both 'reconcilable', according to Milton.

Paradise Lost and its complex questionings of the human condition were twenty-five years away but the divorce tract caused a massive public disputation. In December 1644 Milton was summoned before the House of Lords for examination. According to John Phillips, Milton's other nephew and biographer (Darbishire, p. 24), the case against him was 'soon dismissed'. What exactly this case was remains unclear. In September 1644 Prynne in *Twelve Considerable Serious Questions* had called for the suppression of Milton's pamphlet, accusing it of irreligious liberality, but the legalistic-theological specifics of the case against Milton are lost. In his *Tetrachordon* and *Colasterion* (4th March 1645) Milton vindicates himself not by particularising the case of his accusers but by reinforcing the proposals of his first divorce pamphlet. At the centre of all this are the tensions caused by the religious differences of the period. Milton's accusers were not exclusively Anglo-Catholics (for whom divorce was forbidden and sacrilegious): Prynne, for example, was a Presbyterian. Essentially Milton seemed to be moving towards a radical Arminianist position of free will, in the sense that he interpreted scripture in a way which suggested that intellectual competence was as important as the acceptance of conventional interpretations, irrespective of their allegiance. A subjective and revealing depiction of Milton's perception of all this is available in his Sonnet XII, 'On the Detraction which followed upon my writing of Certain Treatises'. The 'Treatises' referred to are Milton's divorce pamphlets. The sonnet was not published until 1673 but it was circulated in manuscript form when it was written in 1646.

It begins:

I did but prompt the age to quit their clogs
By the known rules of ancient liberty
When straight a barbarous noise environs me
Of owls and cuckoos, asses, apes and dogs.

(1–4)

The Renaissance English sonnet was associated predominantly with a one-to-one relationship between a speaker and listener, usually involving an amatory theme (Shakespeare being the exemplar) or some other intensely personal issue (Donne's so-called 'Holy Sonnets' for example). Milton in his 1640s sequence of sonnets altered this agenda significantly: while retaining an autobiographical scenario these poems usually become vehicles for political dialectic, and this is one of the most acerbic of all.

The animal imagery of the fourth line sums up Milton's opinion of the New Parliamentarians, evoking classical, mainly Ovidian, associations: owl = ignorance; cuckoo = ingratitude and vanity; dog = obtuse quarrelsomeness. These verbal cartoons reflect Milton's anger, but they are underpinned by a more considered treatment of the men who had summoned him to answer for his ideas, focusing on the notion of 'liberty' (line 2). He presents his detractors, mainly the Presbyterian element of Parliament, as those who

> *Bawl for freedom in their senseless mood,*
> *And still revolt when truth would set them free.*
> *License they mean when they cry liberty;*
> *For who loves that, must first be wise and good;*
> *But from that mark how far they rove we see*
> *For all this waste of wealth, a loss of blood.*
>
> (*TP*: 9–14)

By 'license' Milton means dictatorial authoritarianism, as opposed to the ideal of 'liberty'. The latter had been the 'cry', the unifying principle, of the Parliamentarian cause in the war, and in Milton's view requires its advocates to be both 'wise and good'. The 'revolt', he contends, has gone backward; a terrible 'loss of blood' will have been for nothing if the new government cannot accept and institute genuine liberty – in short, to allow the likes of Milton to offer radical ideas in print.

The Battle of Naseby in 1645 was the turning point in the Civil War. Over the previous three years Oliver Cromwell had orchestrated what was the first modern military campaign. He treated his troops as professional soldiers, equipped them well with the most sophisticated armour and weaponry and planned encounters with cold circumspection. His colleague Lord Fairfax became commander-in-chief of this so-called New Model Army. After Naseby, the Royalist forces were reduced to disarray and Oxford, the King's headquarters, surrendered to the Parliamentarians commanded by Fairfax in 1646. Charles fled but was captured a few months later and remained prisoner until his execution in 1649. The final, decisive battle was the siege of Colchester of 1648, at which the remaining, monarchless Royalists were routed by Fairfax's forces.

The years between 1645 and 1649 seem for most biographers of Milton to represent if not quite a hiatus then at least a period of reflection in his career as a writer. Between the two dates he produced no pamphlets. He wrote no more than two brief poems per year, all of which addressed themselves to ongoing civil, political and religious issues. Typically, in Sonnet XI, he returns us to the controversy of the divorce pamphlets (lines 3–6), particularly *Tetrachordon*, which is mentioned in the opening line. He gives the impression that this pamphlet was the mid-seventeenth-century equivalent of a bestseller: 'it walked the town awhile'… (3). More significantly, this is the poem in which Milton comes closest to bombastic satire. The 'stall reader' is confused by the classical roots of *Tetrachordon* ('Bless us! What a word on / A title page is this!' 5–6) and for Milton their reaction is symptomatic of the Presbyterians' refusal to accept open debate; theological absolutism is ranked with philistinism. Milton himself lowers his register, suggesting that the Scottish names 'Gordon, Colkitto, or Macdonnel, or Galasp' are just as obscure but more 'rugged' than his own pamphlet title, and implies that their non-Anglo-Saxon roots testify to a new level of barbarism, names 'that would have made Quintilian stare and gasp' (11). The surnames themselves echo those of known Scots Presbyterians (p. 305). He invokes the presence of 'Sir John Cheke' (12), the first Professor of Greek at Cambridge and one of the most famous English classicists and humanists, implying that the new age of reason and learning ushered in by the likes of Cheke, the Renaissance, is being dismantled by the Presbyterian fundamentalists.

He also worked on his *History of Britain* and a related document called *The Character of the Long Parliament*, which would be published respectively in 1670 and 1681. Both reflect and are consistent with the religious and political ideas of the pamphlets but lack their energy. Perhaps he was more concerned with the new, or rather renewed, experience of married life. Some time, probably during the spring, in 1645 Milton was summoned mysteriously to the house of his friends the Blackboroughs where waiting for him, alone in a back room, he found Mary. Edward Phillips (Darbishire, pp. 66–7) claims that Mary was penitent and submissive, 'begging Pardon on her knees before him'. They were reconciled and she joined him in his new house in the Barbican. Less than a year later their first child, Anne, was born. They would have three more: a son, John (March 1651) and two other daughters, Mary (October 1648) and Deborah (May 1652). Mary senior died two days after the birth of Deborah on 5th May. Childbirth in the seventeenth century was the most frequent cause of death for younger women. Mary was twenty-eight.

Some have averred that Milton's true motive for the divorce tracts was his own wish to exchange Mary, in her absence, for another woman. John Phillips began the rumour, stating that his uncle's wife's return 'put a stop or rather an end to a grand affair, which was more than probably thought to be then in agitation: It was indeed a design of marrying one of Dr Davis's daughters, a very handsome and witty gentlewoman, but averse as it is said to this motion' (Darbishire, p. 23). More recently A.N. Wilson writes as if he personally had witnessed Milton and the mysterious Miss Davis in flagrante:

Poor Milton! ... There really could not have seemed much future in his marriage. As far as Mary was concerned, he must have forgotten what it was like to be in love with her. He was in love with Miss Davis. And the version of his marriage which was easiest, at that date to believe, and easiest to tell Miss Davis, was that he knew that he had made a mistake as soon as the words of the marriage vow were out of his mouth. (p. 145)

Wilson's intention is to reveal Milton as a man swayed more by lust than reason, to show that the subtle intellectual exercises of the divorce tracts are a mere pretext for sorting out his own pitiably messy love life. Wilson, incidentally, is an inflexibly devout Roman Catholic. Nothing for certain is known of the very existence of Miss Davis or her father the doctor. They began life in Phillips' single sentence and as for the authenticity of his account he comes close to admitting that even for him it was nothing more than vague rumour. The 'grand affair' was, he concedes, '*probably thought* to be then in agitation', and as for Miss Davis's reluctance to marry Milton, she was 'averse *as it is said* to this motion'. It seems odd, indeed bizarre, that Phillips, who was a regular visitor to the Barbican house, sometimes a temporary resident during the period when the alleged affair took place, should admit, albeit implicitly, to have never actually encountered Miss Davis nor heard Milton speak of her. Why then does he invent her? Probably because he wished to dress his uncle with a hint of charisma and glamour: in the post-Restoration period when he wrote his biography Milton was often presented as a dour puritan.

After his reconciliation with Mary – their marriage, despite their differences in temperament and disposition, was thereafter by all accounts a happy one – Milton made peace with her family: indeed he effectively rescued her father Richard from bankruptcy. His own father died in March 1647, leaving Milton his various properties and investments: the management of these would involve a further distraction from his writings. Edward Phillips in his biography offers little more than a paragraph on his uncle's intellectual life during the 1645–9 period. He moved from the Barbican to a smaller house in High Holborn: 'Here he liv'd a private and quiet life, still prosecuting his studies and curious search into knowledge, the grand affair perpetually of his life…' (Darbishire, p. 68). One assumes that this echo of his cousin John's notion of another 'grand affair' is purely coincidental.

It was a puzzling time. *Samson Agonistes*, a lengthy pseudo-epic poem on the story of Samson and Delilah, would not be published until 1671, but some, Parker particularly, argue that he was preparing it in the late 1640s. There are biographical parallels. Consider Delilah's speech when she returns to her husband.

> *With doubtful feet and wavering resolution*
> *I come, still dreading thy displeasure, Samson*
> *Which to have merited, without excuse,*
> *I cannot but acknowledge; yet if tears*
> *May expiate (though the fact more evil draw*
> *In the perverse event than I foresaw)*
> *My penance hath but slackened, though my pardon*
> *No way assured. But conjugal affection*
> *Prevailing over fear, and timorous doubt*
> *Hath led me on desirous to behold*
> *Once more thy face, and know of thy estate.*

(732–42)

Was he here recollecting his meeting with Mary in the Blackboroughs' house?

More significantly, Samson was blind, and in the late 1640s Milton was becoming increasingly aware of severe problems with his own eyesight. By 1652 he would become, like Samson, completely blind. Blindness features as a somewhat ghostly yet insistent theme in Milton's life and writing. In 'L'Allegro' and

'Il Penseroso' there is a curious tension between the enjoyment of the perceived world, what could be fully experienced and *seen,* and the contemplative mode, the life of the mind. His meeting with Galileo who had seen and reported a new universe but was by then unable to see anything at all intrigued him. Milton would contemplate the strange, almost ironic, relationship between matters perceived and things known without sight in his 1650s 'blindness' sonnets and in Book II of *Paradise Lost*.

Milton in the Political Centre-Ground

The trial and the execution of Charles I drew Milton back into the maelstrom of English political and religious debate. A few weeks after Charles was beheaded Milton published, in February 1649, a pamphlet called *The Tenure of Kings and Magistrates* which was and has remained a controversial document. It was written during the trial of the king, the progress and details of which Milton is thought to have been aware; and, with only indirect reference to these events, he investigates their premises and contexts. His thesis is that monarchy holds power by virtue of a tacit contract with the people. If the former fails in this stewardship – and Milton suggests, rather than explicitly claims, that Charles had done so – it should be called to account by its subjects. Milton's thesis was not in itself revolutionary or unprecedented. James I, Charles's predecessor, had, thirty years before, produced a document called *Basilikon Doron* in which he acknowledged that monarchy should involve an awareness of and a sympathetic response to the complexities, opinions and uncertainties of the kingdom (Shakespeare's *Measure for Measure* was a dramatic enactment of James's abstractions). However, no nation before this had tried its monarch for his failures, found him guilty and killed him. In one passage Milton – without mentioning Charles by name – conducts what is in effect a case for the prosecution and deserved sentence, arguing that those who practise tyranny must expect the death sentence.

But this I dare owne as part of my faith, that if such a one there be, by whose Commission, whole massachers have been committed on his faithfull Subjects, his Provinces offered to pawn or alienation, as the hire of those whom he had solicited to come in and destroy whole Citties and Countries; be he King, or Tyrant, or Emperour, the Sword of Justice is above him; in whose hand soever is found sufficient power to avenge the effusion and so great a deluge of innocent blood. For if all human power to execute, not accidentally but intendedly, the wrath of God upon evil doers without exceptions, be of God; then that power, whether ordinary, or if that faile, extraordinary so executing that intent of God, is lawfull, and not to be resisted. (*CPW*, III, pp. 197–8)

Milton neither retracted any of the arguments of *The Tenure* nor expressed regret for composing the piece, and passages such as the above were cited by those who, after the restoration of the monarchy, wanted him prosecuted for regicide.

It has sometimes been suspected that, when writing *The Tenure of Kings and Magistrates,* Milton was in contact with members of the republican government-in-waiting, many of whom attended Charles's trial and were signatories to his death warrant. The pamphlet involves such a depth of detail regarding ongoing political developments that his acquaintance with some of the individuals involved seems more than likely. As well as a justification for regicide, the document includes a lengthy attack upon the Presbyterians in the Commons, whom he treats as hypocrites. They who had campaigned energetically against the Royalist party at the beginning of the war now actively denounced those who had decided to prosecute the king. Milton's argument carries a magisterial logic. Men, created in God's image, were 'born free... born to command and not to obey'. Adam's transgression had caused confusion and disarray and it is only now that fallen man can claim to be returning to a state which at least corresponds with his condition before the Fall. None among mankind can claim authority by right; governance shall be determined by a collective sense of justice and reason (pp. 8–11). In short, Milton is citing the Old Testament as justification for the overthrow, indeed the execution, of a monarch who stood against man's attempt to make the best of his post-lapsarian condition. The validity of his thesis is a matter for historians and theologians, but what is particularly striking about it is its relationship to his later, ever-puzzling interpretation of the Old Testament in *Paradise Lost*. He seems in *The Tenure of Kings and Magistrates* to be suggesting that in England, in 1649, fallen man was at last becoming aware of how a diminished but honourable equivalent of his state before the Fall might be implemented in terms of a new political consensus. The Cromwellian, republican Commonwealth, the shadowy precursor to modern democracy, was imminent. By the time *Paradise Lost* went to press in 1667 this project had failed horribly and at the end of the poem the foreseeable prospects for Adam's lineage are informed with far less optimism than can be found in *The Tenure*.

Milton was soon drawn into a practical involvement with contemporary politics. Within a month of the execution of Charles I, the hotchpotch of military leaders, Parliamentarians and unaffiliated supporters of the anti-Royalist cause formed what amounted to the first Republican government in Europe since the days of the Roman Empire. The new Council of State had forty executive members. Parliament endured but the Council effectively became the pro-active force of the nation, procuring for itself the role of initiating policy that Parliament would then endorse, and the power to overrule Parliamentary decisions. Thirty-one of its members were also in Parliament, five were lawyers or judges, three were senior army officers, four were peers and thirteen were signatories of the death sentence upon the king. In May 1649 the Council appointed Milton as its Secretary for Foreign Languages. As he recalled in *Defensio*

Secunda (1654), 'The so-called Council of State, which was then for the first time established by the authority of Parliament, summoned me, though I was expecting no such event, and desired to employ my services, especially in connection with foreign affairs' (*CPW*, IV. 1, pp. 627–8).

No precise record exists regarding Milton's powers and duties. To assume that he was a senior administrator, in modern terms a civil servant, while members of the Council were exclusively responsible for the making of decisions would be to impose a post-eighteenth-century model of governance upon something that was far from certain of its own practices. In practical terms his talents and range as a linguist qualified him for this, but it was known also that Milton's skill as a rhetorician along with his sympathetic affiliations would be of enormous benefit in the Council's early dealings with the rest of Europe: even intrinsically rebellious and unorthodox states such as Holland were variously horrified and confounded by the news of Charles's execution, while others, such as Spain, regarded the act as Satanic.

At the time of his appointment Milton was living in modest quarters in High Holborn but was immediately offered more spacious temporary accommodation in Charing Cross prior to taking up residence in a government-owned house in Scotland Yard, adjacent to Parliament and to Whitehall where the Council met.

His move west, towards the centre of government and away from the City where he had spent most of his life, was symbolic in a number of ways. The divisions between the City and the royal base at Westminster had from the early seventeenth century onwards sown the seeds for the Civil War. By the end of the 1640s these two axes had become a single unit, governed by the victorious anti-monarchists who had taken over the buildings of Parliament and what had once been the royal court as their headquarters. The fact that the Cromwellian Council chose the Banqueting House in Whitehall as the site for the execution of Charles I involved a degree of ruthless calculation. It had been commissioned by his father James to symbolise the strength and grandeur of the new Stuart dynasty, a neo-classical statement of authority over the untidy collection of Tudor and Medieval structures of old Westminster. The axeman, framed by Inigo Jones's Palladian columns, signalled the beginning of something unprecedented.

Though Milton was unflinching in his defence of the new government we have no reliable evidence of how Milton felt about its effects upon his immediate environment, his home. The theatre, as a business and a vehicle for writing, had been the driving force for English Renaissance literature. During the reign of Elizabeth, eleven theatres were opened, all on the periphery of the City, close enough to enable audiences to be drawn from that most densely populated area but safely beyond the reach of clerics who oversaw recreational activities within their parish boundaries. During the 1640s every theatre – and many more had been built in the reigns of James I and Charles I – was pulled down by order of the Council, and open-air performances of plays banned. Their reasons were twofold: ostensibly they were enforcing the beliefs of many radical Puritans that drama by its very nature was a licence for hedonist indulgence and immorality, while a more powerful motive was the fear that uncontrolled assemblies, and the words of the plays themselves, could encourage anti-government, potentially pro-Royalist and pro-Catholic, sedition. Although Milton never referred directly to what was happening in the capital he commented, in 1642, on how he had felt about collegiate play-acting undertaken by his fellow undergraduates in Cambridge almost twenty years earlier:

In the College [they] … have bin seene so oft upon the Stage writhing and unboning their Clergie limes to all the antick and dishonest gestures of Tinrulos', Buffons, and Bawds;… they thought themselves gallant men, and I thought them fools, they made sport, and I laught, they mispronounc't,

and I mislik't, and to make up the *atticisme*, they were out,
and I hist… If it be unlawfull to sit and behold a mercenary
Comedian personating that which is least unseemely for
a hireling to doe, how much more blanefull is it to indure
the sight of as vile things acted by persons either enter'd,
or presently to enter into the ministery.
(*Apology, CPW,* I, pp. 887–8)

One can't help suspecting that he felt the presence of a particularly popular literary predecessor at his back, a man whose most
successful medium had now been officially consigned to the
realm of impropriety.

Through the reigns of Elizabeth, James and Charles the
streets and fields that lay between Westminster and the City,
particularly the Strand, had regularly been sites for parochial
festivals and feastings, a leftover from the days of Catholicism
that had become an excuse for collective enjoyment, where rope
dancers, puppeteers and farceurs would entertain the ordinary
citizens, who would also avail themselves of bread, cheese, ale
and meat from a spit-roasted pig or cow. These too were treated
as cases of exhibitionist dissipation and all but abolished by
the Cromwellian authorities. In their place Ranters, Quakers,
Levellers and representatives of dozens of other sects and parties
competed for space and the attention of an audience in the same
open thoroughfares and parks that had previously drawn people
for days of jollification.

In one other respect the 1640s saw the creation of London as
a single metropolis, at least in the way that we routinely perceive
it. After the first attack on Westminster by Royalist forces in
1642, Parliamentarians set about erecting a vast defence system
of ditches, mounds and more substantial fortified towers. By
May 1643 the Venetian ambassador told of 'forts completed and
admirably designed. They are now beginning the connecting
lines.' This line of defences enclosed the area we now regard as
central London, taking in Whitechapel to the east of the City,

running between Shoreditch and Tyburn Road in the north, and from the west halting on the banks of the Thames at Vauxhall and Kent Street. We cannot be certain of Milton's thoughts on this but he must have been conscious of the fact that the untidy collection of semi-urban, semi-rural centres where he had grown up was now a single unit, the capital of what would soon become the new Commonwealth, with John Milton employed as its principal advocate and defender.

A few weeks after Milton's *Tenure* appeared, a bestseller hit the streets of London. *Eikon Basilike* (literally the 'King's Image', but popularly known as the 'King's Book') was a compilation of prayers, reflections and pietistic meditations allegedly authored by Charles during his imprisonment and trial. No absolute proof of its origin, such as manuscript copies, has ever been produced but at the time its readers did not doubt its authenticity, and there were many readers. The book aroused a popular feeling of abhorrence among the literate public at the apparent murder committed by the Council, in the people's name, of a sensitive, Christian leader. Parliament attempted to suppress it, but failed; its popularity guaranteed its continued production by discreet, unacknowledged presses inside and outside London. It fell to Milton to defend the government, which he did in a book called *Eikonoklastes* ('The Image Breaker'), published in October 1649. *Eikonoklastes* returns to the argument of *Tenure* but with far less restraint. Milton presents the king as a criminal; hedonist, thief, hypocrite, and in his Papal allegiances, traitor. He pitches the argument at a level that he knows will register with the ordinary reader, claiming that much of the *Eikon* is a fabric of plagiarism, with stealings from the work of Sidney and Shakespeare: modified passages from *Richard III* are, Milton states, ironically appropriate, given the parallels between the two monarchs.

An important feature of *Eikonoklastes* is its style, which invites contrast with earlier documents. In *The Reason of Church Government* the prose reflects Milton's optimistic, some might argue naively optimistic, imaginings of the outcome of the Civil

War; it is shamelessly ebullient and energised. *Areopagitica* is more studied and calculating in its manner: by 1644, Milton knew that his idealism was somewhat premature, that he was obliged to address factions and political-religious constituencies that bespoke various levels of extremism, authoritarianism and ambition. Anger and frustration inform *Eikonoklastes.* It reads in one sense as an obligation, a task undertaken by Milton reluctantly, and while we have no reason to doubt the sincerity of his arguments they sometimes remind one of the savage editorials of modern tabloid newspapers, shot through with a blend of political contingency and forced rhetoric. Consider the following passage on the state of the new republic.

> It were a nation miserable indeed, not worth the name of a nation, but a race of idiots, whose happiness and welfare depended on one man [the King]. The happiness of a nation consists in true religion, piety, justice, prudence, temperance, fortitude and the contempt of avarice and ambition. They in whomsoever these virtues dwell eminently, need not kings to make them happy, but are the architects of their own happiness, and whether to themselves or others are not less kings. (*CPW*, p. 254)

Now compare this with the passage from the *Reason of Church Government*, quoted above (p. 67). In the latter the syntax virtually cascades with its author's imaginings, while *Eikonoklastes* reads more like a document prepared by a man who feels obliged to instruct and specify.

The one quite extraordinary occasion on which Milton's erstwhile vocation as a poet and his status as spokesman for the Commonwealth merged occurred in 1655. The Waldenses people existed as a semi-independent religious community on the borders of France and Italy. They had been collectively excommunicated by Rome in 1215 and since the sixteenth century had been regarded by many as the original Protestants.

Indeed, Milton in *Eikonoklastes* celebrates them as the true precursors of the more recent Reformation.

> ...if we may believe what the papists themselves have written of these churches which they call Waldenses, I find it in a book written almost four hundred years since, and set forth in the Bohemian *History* [of Václav Hájek], that those churches in Piedmont have held the same doctrine and government since the time that Constantine with his mischievous donations poisoned Silvester and the whole Church. Others affirm they have so continued there since the Apostles, and Theodorus Belvederensis, in his relation of them, confesseth that those heresies (as he names them) were from the first times of Christianity in that place. (*CPW*, III, p. 514)

On 25th January 1655, Immanuel, Duke of Savoy, issued an ultimatum to the Waldenses of Piedmont ordering them either to convert to Roman Catholicism or to leave the area. They refused to do either and Savoy's forces massacred more than 2,000 people. In May a process of persecution and selective slaughter was still underway and news of these events reached London. Cromwell's Council decided immediately to intervene and Milton was told to compose, translate and despatch letters of protest to the Duke of Savoy and the King of France and requests for military intervention to Sweden, Denmark, Switzerland, Transylvania and the United Provinces.

Soon afterwards the impassioned rhetoric of the letters were distilled by Milton into what must qualify as the most enraged, polemical sonnet in the English language, 'On the Late Massacre in Piedmont':

Avenge, O Lord, Thy slaughtered saints, whose bones
Lie scattered on the Alpine mountains cold –
Even them who kept Thy truth so pure of old

When all our fathers worshipped stocks and stones,
Forget not! In Thy book record their groans,
Who were Thy sheep, and in their ancient fold
Slain by the bloody Piedmontese that rolled
Mother with infant down the rocks. Their moans
The vales redoubled to the hills, and they
To heaven. Their martyred blood and ashes sow
O'er all the Italian fields where still doth sway
The triple tyrant: that from these may grow
A hundredfold, who having learned Thy way
Early may fly the Babylonian woe.

In November 1649 a document called *Defensio Regia Pro Carolo I* ('A Defence of King Charles I') by the celebrated classical scholar Claudius Salmasius appeared in Europe. It was not translated into English probably because it was aimed at the educated classes: a meticulous point-by-point trawl through biblical, theological and classical sources which sought to prove beyond doubt that the execution of Charles involved the overturning of all divine and natural laws. Again Milton was appointed as respondent; his *Pro Populo Anglicano Defensio* ('A Defence of the English People') came out in early 1651 and its title reflects its thesis. The people of England had punished the king because he stood between them and their realisation of the best that could be hoped for in man's attempts to create some counterpart to the world lost after the Fall. Milton matches Salmasius in his citation of sources, indeed ridicules his unscholarly misuse of them, and supplements this with a blend of nationalism and ideological commitment that we usually associate with twentieth- and twenty-first century political discourse; in Milton's presentation, the Cromwellian regime is licensed by scripture, it involves collective responsibility and not the adoration of a debauched figurehead, and the wise, courageous people of England will monitor its implementation of policy.

The consequences of 'the Defence' were considerable. Its reverberations throughout Europe projected Milton from the status of relative obscurity to that of the international acclaim that, as early as 1637, he had confessed to Diodati was his ambition. 'You ask me what I am thinking of? So help me God, an immortality of Fame' (23rd November 1637, *CPW*, I, p. 347). In March 1651 a Dutch translation was commissioned and an immediate order of twenty-five copies placed for the specific scrutiny of members of the government of the Netherlands. In July it was reported that the book had been publicly burned in Toulouse and Paris 'for fear of making State Heretiques'. Later that month the French government declared it an act of treason, punishable by death, 'to print, vend or have it in possession'. It was widely reported, admittedly without verification, that Queen Christina of Sweden 'spoke highly of the genius of the man, and his manner of writing' (*LR*, III, pp. 15–16). The Council itself issued a public announcement of thanks for his achievements.

> The Councel takeing notice of the manie good services performed by Mr John Mylton their Secretarie for forreigne languages to this State and commonwealth particularlie of his booke in Vindication of the Parliament and people of England against the calumnies and invectives of Salmasius, have thought fit to declare their resentment [appreciation] and good acceptance of the same and that the thankes of the Councel bee returned to Mr Mylton, and their sense represented in that behalf (French, III, p. 43).

Milton was becoming, in the public consciousness and professionally, the official spokesman for the fledgling Cromwellian state. Our perception of his private opinions and ideals regarding politics and religion can be assembled from our slight knowledge of what he actually said – Edward Phillips is our principal, though by no means verifiable or trustworthy, source for this –

and what we intuit from his contemporaneous writing. His primary allegiance was to the Independents. Independency involved the belief in Christ as the only true head of the church, and the Bible, variously interpretable, as its only rule for faith. Milton, without using the term, defined Independency as coming 'from the true freedom of Christian doctrine and church-discipline subject to no superior judge but God only' (Hunter, IV, p. 101). Independents treated the individual believer as the sage and determinant of his own theological centre-ground and religious practice. Often they would attach themselves to specific institutions, chiefly the Church of England, but would treat institutionalised religion more as a pragmatic necessity than an organising principle for faith and thought. It could be argued that Independency was the driving force for the early Parliamentarian cause but in the years at the close of the Civil War and during the establishment of a republic, it inevitably involved a paradox: many Independents, now faced with the practicalities of government, were becoming instruments of institutionalization. Milton had addressed these specifics more in his, albeit slight, poetic output of the late 1640s/early 1650s than in his prose writings. In many ways the chronology of these poems reflects his growing sense of unease at the development of the new state. As we have seen, in Sonnet XII (1646) he rails against the objections in Parliament inspired by the Presbyterians to his divorce pamphlets and in 'On the New Forcers of Conscience…' (1646) he names senior Presbyterian clerics and theologians as the Protestant versions of Catholic authoritarians.

Colchester, one of the last towns to be held by the Royalists, fell on 27th August 1648 and 'On the Lord General Fairfax at the Siege of Colchester' was written shortly afterwards. It celebrates the military career of Fairfax, arguably the most skilled and effective general on the Parliamentarian side. The Civil War was effectively over but Milton refers to 'new rebellions' which 'raise/their hydra heads' (6–7). The Homeric beast with nine heads embodies the sense of there still being numerous threats to the Parliamentarian ascendancy: principally the Royalist uprisings in Kent and Wales and the Scots invasion from the north. Fairfax, implies Milton, would play the role of Hercules and slay the beast.

The sestet (closing six lines) of the sonnet is important because it states that 'yet a nobler task awaits thy hand' (9). Milton suggests that Fairfax should, in effect, take command of peacetime England. Milton admired him as a man of balanced conviction, a figure who would at once temper the extremism of the Presbyterians and impose a version of military discipline upon the variously corrupt and anarchistic elements among the disunited victors. In fact after the war Fairfax retired from public life (he eventually came to express remorse for the execution of the king), which might explain Milton's decision to leave the poem out of his 1673 volume: it appeared in print after Milton's death, in 1694.

The poem reflects Milton's anger while being lit by a confident, inspired sense of Independency, particularly his own, as able to resist the power of religious factionalism. However, his praise of Fairfax is touched by a sense of anxiety and Milton implores him to save the fledgling state from threats both internal and external, and not only from remaining Royalists. 'To the Lord General Cromwell' is virtually a rerun of its predecessor. When it was written, in 1652, Cromwell had replaced Fairfax as the most eminent military tactician on the Parliamentarian side (he would not become Lord Protector until 1653) and, like the Fairfax sonnet, the octave (first eight lines) celebrates its subject's brilliance as a general. Cromwell had commanded the armies which defeated the Scots, first at Preston in 1648 – 'While Darwen stream with blood of Scots imbrued' (7) – then at Worcester in 1651 (9). Again the sestet shifts the emphasis to the subject's peacetime role: 'yet much remains to conquer still... new foes arise/Threatening to bind our souls with secular chains' (9–12). The 'new foes' are generally taken to be those who argued in Parliament for a reformulated established church with limited tolerance of dissenters. The 'Committee for Propagation of the Gospel' had been set up to oversee these matters and Cromwell was a member. Milton had argued in *Areopagitica* for unrestricted liberty of speech and worship and in the 1650s campaigned for the practical implementation of these ideals within the new republic. The fact that Milton's views proved to be more radical than those of the eventual Cromwellian regime is probably the reason why this sonnet, like its predecessor, remained out of print until 1694. It was outspoken and radical to an extent that would not have gained its author much sympathy during the Restoration. He asks Cromwell to stand against Members of Parliament, mainly Presbyterians, who were campaigning for the reorganisation of an established church which would exclude dissidents in much the same way as the Pro-Catholic High Church of Charles had done, albeit according to an antithetical core doctrine.

After Fairfax and Cromwell comes Vane, the third figure in whom Milton invests his hopes for the future of England. In 1652, when 'To Sir Henry Vane the Younger' was written, the first naval skirmishes in the eventual war between England and Holland took place (even Holland, one of the most solidly Protestant European states, had taken issue at the execution of Charles I). Vane had become, in effect, foreign minister in the Council of State and the octave urges him to 'unfold/the drift of hollow states' (5–6), 'hollow' being part-pun on Holland, part-reference to its physical 'state' below sea level, part-condemnation of its moral hollowness or inconsistency. As usual, the sestet shifts the frame of reference to the condition of England and Vane is presented as a figure competent 'to know/Both spiritual power and civil, what each means./What savers each. Thou hast learned, which few have done' (9–11). Once more emphasis is given to Milton's hoped-for republic, in this case where 'civil' and 'spiritual' (religious) power will remain separate, and to the sonnet's subject as one of its leaders. Vane was allied with the

Independents, and, like Milton, he was utterly opposed to an established church. Although he did not support the king's execution he was excluded from the Act of Indemnity and executed in January 1662. Milton, bravely, allowed this sonnet to be printed in Sike's *Life and Death of Sir Henry Vane* later that same year. These three poems were circulated in manuscript form among Milton's friends, colleagues and seniors, including Fairfax, Cromwell and Vane. As such they offer an insight into his personal opinions on the state of government. He was and would remain an Independent, an advocate of the fundamental rights of free speech and manner of worship. However, he was himself being drawn more into the practicalities of government in which idealism and circumstantial necessity were rarely the same thing.

In 1649 the Parliamentarian government had employed a small army of scribes to set on paper the immense output of this now near-blind political and religious theorist. He had been appointed as author of the so-called *Observations*, a year-by-year explanation and justification of government policy, in which Milton employed his rhetorical skills to deal with such issues as Cromwell's Irish campaign and the imprisonment of the more active members of such republican splinter groups as the Diggers and Levellers. These, particularly the Diggers, advocated a political system that was close to modern democracy. Gerrard Winstanley, the leader of the Diggers, pre-empted socialism in his call for the common ownership of land. During the late 1640s the Diggers, directed by Winstanley, took possession of vast acreages of common and open land in Surrey, Buckinghamshire, Kent and Northamptonshire. They set up communes in which basic services such as smithing and tailoring along with agricultural produce would be distributed free within the locality, and the Bible was cited as the pretext for these new forms of social organisation. The government in London appeared to approve in that they neither criticised nor sought to actively undermine the Diggers' experiments. But when, in 1650, local landowners sent in armed thugs to disperse the communes the Council declined to intervene, despite fervent pleas from Winstanley and others.

In 1651 Milton's duties were supplemented by his appointment as Chief Censor, a magnificently ironic choice on the part of the government given that central to practically all of Milton's pro-republican writings was his belief in and defence of free speech. He was, to say the least, a libertarian censor; only those publications which directly incited the overthrow of the government were suppressed. Indeed he permitted the publication of *The Moderate,* the argumentative news-sheet of the Levellers, which continually called for the empowerment of the common people. He co-edited the official government newspaper called *Mercurius Politicus*, the mid-seventeenth-century equivalent of the Thatcherite *Sun* and *Times* of the 1980s. It could be argued that the office of Censor in the Cromwellian Commonwealth was perceived, not least by its occupant, more in its original classical specification as a person who comments upon and engages with the opinions and conduct of others than in its modern sense of a figure who licenses or bans publications. London teemed with newspapers and pamphleteering was reaching crescendo proportions. John Lilburne, the most vocal, fanatical spokesman for the Levellers, published pieces advocating that Parliament should reform itself and provide representation for the seventeenth-century forerunners of the working classes, the artisans, yeomen and craftsmen who existed in a political vacuum. The Presbyterians, outside Parliament, counted among their number some of the best pamphleteers in the country.

Milton lasted little more than a year as Chief Censor. In late 1652 he had licensed the publication of a notorious, heretical tract called the *Racovian Catechism*, which amongst other things denied the doctrine of the Trinity. The Council was unsettled and summoned Milton to justify his act. He stated to them that he was enacting his own principles of free speech, specified in *Areopagitica* and elsewhere, and in effect resigned. He would continue as Latin Secretary, officially, until 1655 when his blindness and other commitments had caused these duties to become impractical. He did not completely give up his activities as the Council's international representative and a compromise was agreed. His salary of £288 was reduced to a life pension of £150 and in return for this he would be available to the Council if his skills were required. He would remain so until the Restoration of the Monarchy in 1660.

Milton's most fascinating work of the mid-1650s was the *Defensio Secunda* ('The Second Defence'), published in 1654. Nominally at least this was a continuation of the exchange between Milton and Salmasius, with this response seemingly provoked by a tract published anonymously in The Hague and entitled *Regia Sanguinis Clamor ad Coelum Adversus Parricidas Anglicanas* ('The Cry of the Royal Blood to Heaven Against the English Parricides') (1652). Prominent members of the Council are picked out as villains but the anonymous author of the *Clamor* (which was originally attributed to one Alexander More but was later admitted to after the Restoration by an English Royalist Pierre du Moulin) is obsessively preoccupied with Milton. Hardly a page passes without him being presented as physically repugnant and intellectually and morally inferior: '"A monster horrible, deformed, huge and sightless." Though to be sure he is not huge; nothing more weak, more bloodless, more shrivelled than little animals such as he' (*CPW*, IV. 2, p. 1045) who was 'expelled from his college at Cambridge because of some disgrace... [and] fled shame and his country and migrated to Italy'. This 'ignoble, commonplace little fellow', this 'great stinking pestilence', 'swindler' and 'foolish shrew mouse' (pp. 1078–80), is, accuses the author, responsible for the destruction of the institution of marriage through his own foul behaviour to his wife and subsequent divorce tracts and is worse even than the 'parricides' who signed the warrant, given that his documents before the trial had licensed the crime by reviling the sacred nature of kingship (pp. 1050–1).

The *Defensio Secunda* might be expected to amount to a rigorous counter-attack against these allegations and insults, but it is a far more complex and, it must be said, puzzling document. It is a mixture of a panegyric – for Cromwell and others – autobiographical self-scrutiny and reflections on what England had become and what it might yet achieve.

During the period between 1650 and 1655 England hung between the kind of state that might have seemed radical and reformist by early twentieth-century standards and one that threatened a return to various degrees of pre-Civil War authoritarianism. The king was dead but many of his supporters had not officially surrendered; pockets of resistance against republicanism were making their presence felt, particularly in the Western counties. The Battle of Worcester involved a sequence of encounters between the forces of the Protectorate and Royalists, including Scots Presbyterians, which did not conclude until late 1651. Up to December 1651 members both of Parliament and the Council, Cromwell included, were still considering a settlement with 'something of monarchical power'. Who would fill the office of monarch and what powers they would hold remained unanswered questions. The settlement did not get beyond a hypothesis and it only came to that through the reluctant acceptance of the debaters that something might be needed to assuage the vengeful embitterment of the Royalists. At the other end of the spectrum Lilburne, again at large, and other Levellers continued to produce pamphlets calling for unprecedented forms of religious liberty and political governance. In 1652 Winstanley presented to Cromwell a document called *The Law of Freedom in Platform* which envisaged England as a Utopia, a heaven on earth in which all divisions by rank, class, wealth or position would be removed and every citizen would play some role in the management and future of the nation. He argued that the abolition of property and wages would bring with it the extinction of the main causes of wrongdoing, covetousness, envy and greed. Crime and punishment would be minimised and posts such as the parish constable would no longer be necessary. It was, in effect, a Christian *Communist Manifesto*, two centuries before the humanist version would appear. It would never be implemented but the fact that Cromwell himself, to whom it was addressed, formally received a copy, and the censor, Milton, with the sanction of the Council, approved it for distribution and debate indicates the extraordinarily liberal mood of the time.

The continued strength of Cromwell's army halted the attempts by English and Scots Presbyterians to gain control of an established church and to impose their beliefs upon the civil state and as a consequence England became, for the first time in European history, a forum for uncensored debate on the nature of politics and religion. Quakers' meetings became unmonitored seminars in which preachers were sidelined by any members of the congregation who wished to voice their own opinions on the meaning of scripture and the destiny of mankind. The so-called Ranters sect claimed for their followers complete exemption from all moral principles, irrespective of their basis, and the ultra-radical preachers Lodowick Muggleton and John Reeve proclaimed that they themselves were the witnesses prophesied in the Book of Revelation. Milton and Cromwell were ardent supporters of Independency and religious toleration but the freedoms held as justification for the Civil War seemed now to verge upon anarchy. Cromwell decided that the ongoing Parliament would be dissolved on 3rd November 1654 and that in the interim something resembling a Constitution should be decided upon, including the character of the next Parliament, the power and number of its members, and the nature of the electorate and the relationship between church and state. In actuality, however, the unsettled indeterminate nature of government, with Parliament constantly in a condition of flux and Cromwell and others on the Council exercising control, continued until 1660, but the notion of there being a deadline for the birth of the new republic was as much the impetus for *Defensio Secunda* as its apparent status as a reply to the *Clamor*. The first section of it is effectively Milton's auto-biography. Parts of this are clearly rebuttals of the *Clamor* author's accusations, from his claim that Milton was expelled from Cambridge in disgrace to his attacks on him as a pamphlet-eer. But it is far more elaborate and reflective than one would expect from a declaration of self-defence. It reads like the testi-mony of a man who knows that one part of his life is almost concluded; he could be saying goodbye to the figure whose voca-tion, to become an apologist for a new victorious cause, has drawn to a close.

> Ugly I have never been thought by anyone, to my know-ledge... I admit that I am not tall, but my stature is closer to the medium than to the small. Yet what if it were small, as in the case with so many men of the greatest worth in both peace and war? ... I was not ignorant of how to han-dle or unsheathe a sword, nor unpractised in using it each day. Girded with my sword, as I generally was, I thought myself equal to anyone, though he was far more sturdy, and I was fearless of any injury that one man could inflict on another. Today I possess the same spirit, the same strength, but not the same eyes. And yet they have as much the appearance of being uninjured, and are as clear and bright, without a cloud, as the eyes of men who see most keenly... In my face... still lingers a colour exactly opposite to the bloodless and pale, so that although I am past forty, there is scarcely anyone to whom I do not seem younger by about ten years. (*CPW*, IV, pp. 82–3)

Despite such bursts of candour he remains reserved on such matters as his habits and tastes. Did he, we wonder, embody any of the customs most frequently associated with the republicans and their more puritanical religious associates? Toland describes him as 'affable in Conversation, of an equal and cheerful Temper, and highly delighted with all sorts of Music, in which he was himself not meanly skil'd. He was extraordinary temperat in his Diet, which was any thing in season or the easiest procur'd, and was no friend to sharp or strong Liquors' (Darbishire, p. 194). Several of his early biographers remark on his avoidance of 'strong' drink but this is more likely a matter of taste than of principle. Neither Calvin nor Luther advocated temperance, and wine and beer were routinely consumed in London as tastier, and healthier, alternatives to the generally filthy water. The principal 'strong Liquors' were whisky and gin, which are probably what Milton's biographers refer to. According to Edward Phillips, we should not perceive him as constitutionally dour or sullen. When he kept a house at Aldersgate Street, before he married, 'once in three Weeks or a Month he would drop into the Society of some Young Sparks of his Acquaintance, the chief whereof were Mr. *Alphrey* and Mr. *Miller*, two Gentlemen of *Gray's*-Inn, the *Beau's* of those Times, but nothing near so bad as those now-a-days; with these Gentlemen he would make fair bold [and] now and then keep a Gawdy-day' (Darbishire, p. 62). Such 'Gawdy Days' were the free-for-alls of games, feasting and dancing which took place on the common land adjacent to the Inns and which were all but abolished during the Commonwealth.

London had changed and in a lengthy encomium to Cromwell, which presents him not in a hagiographic manner but as a flawed human being responsible for guiding the nation to its proper destiny, Milton addresses his fellow citizens, urging them to accept and deal heedfully with their new state of freedom and, he stresses, responsibility.

[T]o be free is precisely the same as to be pious, wise, just, and temperate, careful of one's property, aloof from another's, and thus finally to be magnanimous and brave, so to be the opposite to these qualities is the same to be a slave. And by the customary judgment and, so to speak, just retaliation of God, it happens that a nation which cannot rule and govern itself, but has delivered itself into slavery as to its own lusts, is enslaved also to other masters whom it does not choose… You, therefore, who wish to remain free, either be wise at the outset or recover your senses as soon as possible. If to be a slave is hard, and you do not wish it, learn to obey right reason, to master yourselves. Lastly, refrain from factions, hatreds, superstitions, injustices, lusts, and rapine against one another. Unless you do this with all your strength you cannot seem either to God or to men, or even to your recent liberators, fit to be entrusted with the liberty and guidance of the state and the power of commanding others, which you arrogate to yourselves so greedily. (*CPW*, IV, p. 684)

Certainly, the passage, and the tract as a whole, is informed by confidence and optimism yet this is offset by a hint that the tasks facing the victors of the Civil War have certainly not been completed.

By 1656 the Foreign Tongues Secretariatship had effectively been taken over by Andrew Marvell, while Milton, in deference to his classical learning, still held prominence regarding important communications in Latin (Marvell would replace Milton as the Latinist in 1657). Marvell had become Milton's assistant three years earlier, and their subsequent relationship is enshrined in the folklore of literary biography. Marvell's most debated, if not most famous, poem is his 'Horatian Ode Upon Cromwell's Return from Ireland' (1650). It is an ambiguous piece, an implementation of ambiguity more as a tactically propitious device than as an intellectual-poetic exercise. It celebrates Cromwell, with whom Marvell was personally acquainted, but it also in a shadowy manner acknowledges the disturbing resonances of the act of king killing. Few facts are known about the friendship between Milton and Marvell, but, as the clichés have it, opposites attract, and Marvell's 'Ode' indicates a great deal. Marvell was a pragmatist, a man whose beliefs and opinions were at once genuine and adaptable to circumstances. He knew that the concept of monarchy was not something that could be suddenly transformed into collective republicanism.

In Marvell's poem the stanza most frequently cited involves Charles's much-reported demeanour at his execution.

He nothing common did or mean
Upon that memorable scene.

Had Milton read these lines when he wrote the *Defensio Anglicano*, his justification for regicide and republicanism published a year later? In the final page of it there is a sentence which almost cites Marvell's poem, and, as it does so, shifts the focus from the executed king to the people of England.

After so glorious a deed, you ought to think, you ought to do nothing that is mean and petty, nothing but what is great and sublime.

Milton's 'you ought' is addressed to the collective consciousness of the nation; he believed that his readers could accept his own perception of the execution as a 'glorious' and 'sublime' step towards the implementation of religious and political freedom. He was an idealist. Marvell was a Machiavellian pragmatist; he remained on good terms with the quietened but still powerful Royalist factions, and after the Restoration profited from this. After 1660, when the monarchy was restored, he would use his political contacts – he would then be Member of Parliament for Hull – to rescue his old friend Milton from the vengeful punishments visited upon many of the regicides.

No one is certain when Milton began *Paradise Lost*, the poem that will forever guarantee his status as one of the great English poets, but it is possible to connect incidents from his life with this work's at once puzzling and universalised message.

Some time in the mid-1650s, when his work for the government was becoming less burdensome, Milton began to assemble a document known as *De Doctrina Christiana*. It would not be published in his lifetime and indeed no one was certain of its existence until it was discovered in manuscript form in the Public Records Office in 1823. Even after it went into print in 1825 some doubted its authenticity; it was difficult, even under the relatively enlightened ethos of the early nineteenth century, to accept that Milton had contemplated such heretical, wayward, deviant thoughts. The parallels between *De Doctrina Christiana* and *Paradise Lost* would have been evident to anyone familiar with both, but the implications of accepting that the former was a rehearsal for the latter were too unsettling to be addressed publicly until the twentieth century (See Kelley, 1941).

Paradise Lost has endured as a controversial work because it involves a cautious, respectful transcription of the book of Genesis alongside very radical questionings of what it meant to John Milton. *De Doctrina Christiana* discloses the origins of these questionings. It deals with familiar doctrinal and theological issues, but in a manner that would not become licensed until the end of the eighteenth century: rationalism, empiricism and individuality threaten the sovereignty of immutable absolutes. God is treated by Milton almost as a person; his motives, objectives and inclinations become unnervingly actual and contingent: there are parallels with Arminianism but it goes much further. For example, early in *De Doctrina* (*WJM*, XIV, pp. 24–6) Milton asks why God created man, not in the characteristically Socratic-theological manner of someone who has foreknowledge of the answer, but as someone who is engaging in an ongoing exchange with God. Did God know that Adam and Eve would fall of their own free will? If so, should we question his love for us, given that he knew in advance of our fate? Yes and no, answers Milton, because while God could foresee the future of man he could not determine it: that this is up to us 'in the exercise of [our] uncontrolled liberty' (p. 82). Milton's encounters in his youth with Calvinist notions of predestination and their antitheses are in

the background, but he has moved beyond stark dichotomies towards a more complex yet flexible engagement with belief. He deals with contradictions, inconsistencies – Adam's 'fall was… certain, but not necessary; it proceeded from his own free will, which is incompatible with necessity' (pp. 82–6) – but he does not attempt to resolve them; they are, he implies, part of our inheritance, our condition, a state that we should contemplate and further investigate.

Throughout the document Milton engages with scripture as though he is conversing with God and offers his own perceptions of what God has been and is doing, and how we should accommodate these notions. Milton declares his anti-Trinitarianism; God is one person, irrespective of the faulty conception of him as Father, Son and Holy Spirit. We, as the inheritors of the Fall, can only properly understand Good because we have become aware of Evil; our understanding of Redemption is consequent upon this. Monogamy is the ideal condition, but compatibility is a fact; divorce is acceptable in that it enables individuals to locate a more secure enactment of marital harmony. He even implies that, since there is no record of God forbidding polygamy, it should perhaps be permitted. (This was the feature of *De Doctrina* which most disturbed the early Victorian sceptics – surely our most eminent Christian poet could not be suggesting that God would approve of promiscuity?) The issue that Milton wrestles with throughout this curious work establishes it primarily as an exploratory preface to his forthcoming epic poem. He wonders again and again if it is possible for man to claim sufficient knowledge of God to imagine his feelings and motives. In short he asks: is God sufficiently similar to man for the latter to represent him in human terms, as indeed Milton would attempt to do.

It is safest for us to form an image of God in our minds

which corresponds to his representation and description of himself in the sacred writings. Admittedly, God is always described or outlined not as he really is but in such a way as will make him conceivable to us. Nevertheless, we ought to form just such a mental image of him as he, in bringing himself within the limits of our understanding, wishes us to form... In short, God either is or is not really like he says he is. If he really is like this, why should we think otherwise? If he is not really like this, on what authority do we contradict God? If, at any rate, he wants us to imagine him in this way, why does our imagination go off on some other tack? (*CPW*, p. 133, p. 136)... We ought not to imagine that God would have said anything or caused anything to be written about himself unless he intended that it should be a part of our conceptions of him. On the question of what is or what is not suitable for God, let us ask for no more dependable authority than God himself. If *Jehovah repented that he had created man*, Gen. vi.6, *and repented because of their groanings,* Judges, ii. 18, let us believe that he did repent... If *he grieved in his heart,* Gen. vi.6, and if, similarly, *his soul was grieved,* Judges x.16, let us believe that he did feel grief... If it is said that God, after working for six days, *rested and was refreshed,* Exod. xxxi. 17, and if he *feared his enemy's displeasure,* Deut. xxxii.27, let us believe that it is not beneath God to feel what grief he does feel, to be refreshed by what refreshes him, and to fear what he does fear ... After all, if *God is said to have created man in his own image, after his own likeness,* Gen. i.26, and not only his mind but also his external appearance (unless the same words mean something different when they are used again in Gen. v.3, *Adam begot his son after his own likeness, in his own image*), and if God attributes to himself again and again a human shape and form, why should we be afraid of assigning to him something he assigns to himself, provided we believe that what is imperfect and weak in us is, when ascribed to God, utterly perfect and utterly beautiful? (*CPW*, pp. 134–6)

We should supplement these questions that Milton addressed to himself with one of our own: how Milton's own life and experiences during the 1650s would influence his ongoing conceptions of God and the human condition. He had witnessed, been part of, events in Christian Europe that were unprecedented, almost apocalyptic. Monarchs were and had always been perceived as the secular agencies of God, but England had shifted the focus.

The Cromwellian republic was founded upon the principle that the nation, not the king, would organise itself, with the assistance of its wisest servants, according to its own conception of God's will. Sadly, and evidently to Milton, this ideal was falling apart. The Cromwellian regime, by the late 1650s, was riven with uncertainty, contradiction and factionalism. Cromwell himself, who had begun his political and military career as the representative of a collective endeavour, was becoming a dictator. Gone was the plain black suit and hat, to be replaced by thick purple robes and the ornaments of magisterial high office: while he kept the title of Lord Protector of the Commonwealth, his wife became Her Highness the Lady Elizabeth. Most of Milton's official duties had by the late 1650s been taken over by Marvell and others (in 1658 a young scholar and poet called John Dryden would become one of Marvell's assistants), but he was still called upon as scripteur and translator of government documents. Informally, his advice was regularly sought and he remained in close contact with those at the centre of power.

The most unsettled, and for those involved unsettling, period of the rapidly fragmenting Commonwealth involved the closing three months of 1659, specifically 13th October to 26th December. During this period the so-called Rump Parliament was dissolved. It is not clear why the dissolution was decided upon given that for all Parliament's faults – principally the various, irreconcilable factions preventing it from acting decisively – its suspension created a vacuum and the potential for catastrophe. Monck commanded the largest army group but it was Major General John Lambert who had raised a force of Civil War veterans and who was responsible for physically enforcing the suspension of Parliament on 13th October. During November Monck, voicing open support for the continuation of the Rump, advanced on London and a third Civil War seemed likely. This prospect was first addressed in print in a short manifesto entitled *Proposalls of Certaine Expedients for the Preventing of a Civill War now Feard, and the Setling of a Firme Government*. Its author was John Milton and if we assume that its content is a formalisation of debates and propositions taking place in the turbulent political forum involving soldiers and politicians then Milton was during those months playing the multiple roles of intermediary, arbitrator and contriver.

He even calls up the most deeply embedded strand of English patriotism. Some populist insurrectionists had during the Civil War associated the Cromwellians with the somewhat mythical notions of Anglo-Saxon freedom and individuality suppressed by the Norman invaders. Milton calls for Parliament to be remodelled as a democratic version of the Roman Senate, and invokes the spirit of Anglo-Saxon independence.

> Because the name of parlament is a Norman or French word, a monument of our Ancient Servitude, commonly held to consist necessarily of 3 Estates, King, Lords, & commons; & the two latter to be called by the King to parlie with him about the great affairs of his realme, it might be very agreeable with our freedome to chang the name of parliament (especially now having outlived its honour by soe many dissolucions) into the name of a Grand or Supreme Counsell. (*CPW*, VII, p. 337)

Milton's two final lengthy treatises of the republic were *Of Civil Power* and *The Likeliest Means to Remove Hirelings*. Both forcefully reiterate the principles of his earlier pamphlets, giving particular emphasis to the notion of free will as the essential predeterminant for the right of the individual regarding the church and the state. Again, he advocates religious liberty, the disestablishment of religious authority from state power, marriage as a reflection of love and companionship rather than merely a legal institution, the right to divorce where the former failed, and the protection of free speech, and the right to publish, against official interference. In the closing sentence of *The Likeliest Means* one senses that he was already aware that any hope of implementing these ideals was fading, that his was a voice in the wilderness. 'If I be not heard nor believed, the event will be my witness to have spoken truth: and I in the mean while have borne my witness not out of season to my church and to my countrey' (*CPW*, VII, p. 321).

Nothing so radical would be publicly voiced again for more than a century, notably in the Constitution of the newly formed United States of America. It was on his part a courageous gesture. He could not be certain of what exactly would replace Cromwell's experiment but he knew that by 1658, after the death of Cromwell, those who wished to revenge themselves against the republicans, and the regicides, would soon occupy positions of power. Among Parliamentarians, particularly the Presbyterians, the restoration of the monarchy was being openly talked of.

In 1658 he wrote what would be his last sonnet, no. XIX, in which he tells of being visited by the spirit of his late wife – though of which one, Mary Powell or the recently departed Katherine Woodcock (m. 1656, d. 1658), we cannot be certain.

Of Milton's three wives we know the least of Katherine Woodcock. It is likely that he never *saw* her. His blindness had become almost complete when they met. Their marriage lasted barely fifteen months. After her death on 3rd February 1658 their daughter, Katherine, born 19th October 1657, followed her; she died for reasons unrecorded on 17th March 1658. The funeral of Mary, his first wife, was unremarkable and largely unrecorded but we know more of Katherine's because of the lavish attention and expense Milton gave to it. She was buried in the grand church of St Margaret's, Westminster. Milton spent £2.13s.4d. on 'right taffety escouti', her coffin being decorated in the manner of a deceased aristocrat. He seemed obsessed with ensuring her complete privacy, specifying that the casket should have twelve locks with twelve different keys. Each of these would be held by specified friends of his until she was interred, undisturbed, in St Margaret's.

In Sonnet XIX he has 'Full sight of her in heaven without restraint', but who, we wonder, is 'her'? The line is loaded with self-focused irony – he now had 'full sight' only of memories. Just before he can 'embrace' this ghostly figure, reality intervenes:

I waked, she fled, and day brought back my night.

The resonant density of this line might move even the most cynical reader of Milton. He seems to exist in a world comprised only of personal, recalled images: everything else is pure darkness. He is remembering, perhaps, not only his late beloved Mary and Katherine but an all-encompassing, almost visionary enterprise. Cromwell too had recently died and the broader vision he once embodied seemed also to be departing. The dream had involved a particular person, but for Milton another dream had died.

The fact that *De Doctrina Christiana* would remain as a collection of incomplete drafts reflects its status as an internalised, personalised expression of Milton's ideas and reflections. It is informed by a sense of isolation, of a man whose perceptions of God and how God's will could be implemented practically by man had been overtaken by events that would destroy them. An epic, involving a literary representation of the book of Genesis and addressing the question as to why we are as we are, had always been a possibility – evidenced by the abandoned

Adam Unparadised. During the 1650s Milton had virtually exchanged his identity as a poet for that of political theorist and theologian, and the fragmentary nature of the prose *De Doctrina* indicates that he was thinking again of making verse his medium, his focus. He had begun *Paradise Lost*.

The Restoration

Frequently, regimes instilled by revolution die a natural death. The radical fervour that brought about the transformation of France at the end of the eighteenth century and Russia at the beginning of the twentieth was in both cases replaced by combinations of stagnation and corruption followed by decay. The Cromwellian Commonwealth established the precedent for this, and by the closing years of the 1650s even ardent republicans were prepared to concede defeat, although what exactly would replace their venture was still a matter for speculation.

Richard Cromwell had briefly replaced his father, but by 1659–60 it was apparent to everyone that the fate of the nation would be determined by General George Monck, who commanded the army. In April 1660, Monck, who had for five years been governor of Scotland, brought his forces south and this time met with no resistance from Lambert or any other military leader. He took control of a directionless bureaucracy of government (Richard Cromwell had already been forced to resign by Monck's London-based military colleagues) and a month later, Charles II, after twelve years of exile, rode into London as the new king. John Evelyn wrote of 'A triumph of above 20,000 horse and foote... brandishing their swords and shouting with inexpressible joy; the ways strewed with flowers, the bells ringing, the streets hung with tapestry, the fountains running with wine; the Major, Aldermen, and all the Companies in their liveries, chaines of gold, and banners; Lords and Nobles clad in cloth of silver, gold and velvet; the windows and balconies well set with ladies.' Evelyn, a Catholic sympathiser who had fought with Charles's forces in the Civil War, might be excused a degree of gratified hyperbole. There was some public rejoicing, but no violence: it seemed to all who witnessed the event, pro- and anti-monarchists, inevitable.

The regime of Charles II would be different from those of his predecessors. The centre of power had shifted irrevocably toward Parliament, but, nevertheless, the ardent monarchists took revenge for what they regarded as a decade of injustice. Several members of the Cromwellian Council were tried by Parliament and executed and Milton, as the most prominent apologist for regicide and republicanism, had to go into hiding. Edward Phillips: 'His next remove was, by advice of those who wished him well and had concern for his preservation, into a place of retirement and abscondence, till such time as the current of affairs for the future should instruct him what farther course to take; it was a friend's house in Bartholomew Close...' (Darbishire, p. 74). We know nothing for certain of who the 'friend' was but it is on record that Dr Theodore Diodati, the late Charles's father, kept a house in the Close until the mid-1650s, so perhaps 'a friend of a friend' would be a more accurate description of Milton's protector. The cause of his flight is clear enough. In June 1660 the Commons, now made up of a solid majority of Royalists, began voting to exclude named persons from a new Bill called the Act of Free and General Pardon, Indemnity and Oblivion. This bizarre procedure involved what amounted to prejudgement, in that, during much of the summer that year, a large number of individuals were arrested, charged with various offences – generally associated with regicide – and speedily sentenced. There were no not-guilty verdicts and all concerned were aware that the legal procedures were formalities. Only if they were put forward under the terms of the Bill as exempt could anyone even remotely associated with the Cromwellian

Commonwealth be certain that sergeants-at-arms would not call without warning. Men with whom Milton worked – notably Major Generals John Lambert, John Desborough, Charles Fleetwood, Thomas Harrison, Speaker of the Commons William Lenthall and Milton's personal friend Sir Henry Vane – were arrested during these months, sentenced to death and a number publicly executed. The manner of these executions was meticulously planned to bring to the victim as much pain and humiliation as possible and to strike fear into those still abroad and uncharged. Major General Harrison was one of the first to be 'hanged by the neck, and being alive cut down, [his] privy members be cut off... entrails taken out of [his] body, and, living, the same be burnt before [his] eyes'. Harrison did not witness his own subsequent beheading, the quartering of his body and distribution of its parts through the city but the court made sure that prior to the event he had a detailed itinerary of all that awaited him. In June 1660 Parliament declared that Milton's *Defensio pro populo Anglicano* and *Eikonoklastes* should be publicly burned and in August licensed the burning, by the official hangman, of all of his available works in print. The Act of Indemnity was passed by both Houses of Parliament on 28th August and signed by the king the following day. One hundred and two persons were named as exempt. Seventy-three others were found guilty of treason without trial and sentenced to death. Twenty-four of these were already dead but Parliament confiscated their estates. Among these, Cromwell himself, Henry Ireton, who had presided at the trial of Charles I, and Milton's friend John Bradshaw had been interred in Westminster Abbey, and Parliament, frustrated, passed a further Act to have their bodies removed, hanged and beheaded and what remained of their already decaying corpses left to rot in the open air. Following the required bureaucratic process these gruesome events were eventually discharged in January 1661.

Milton, having been named neither as exempt nor accused, assumed that he had not been considered for arrest and came out of hiding in early September. Friends arranged for him a temporary lodging in the Red Lion Inn, Holborn. While there, he would have encountered some of the numerous publications put into circulation when he was in hiding which presented him variously as conniving in the murder of the king, as a traitor and an enemy of the state. One of the most popular public poems of the year, the anonymous *Britain's Triumph* (14th May), was a lavish celebration of the Restoration which left room for denunciation of all the most prominent Cromwellians and advised Milton to commit suicide and spare the state, or the mob, the efforts of having him 'stabbed, hang'd, or drown'd'. He would then 'rail no more against his *King*', implying that his *Tenure*, despite being published after the execution, caused him to be as guilty as those who tried and sentenced Charles I. Such material probably prompted one James Norfolke, sergeant-at-arms of the Commons, to assume that there was still a de facto case against Milton. Norfolke and his men arrested him in late September.

His release on 15th December was brought about through the influence of a number of individuals. Milton's brother Christopher had sided with the Royalists during the war and his affiliations were not altered by a decade of republicanism. He had by 1660 become a successful barrister and his promotion to the judiciary on 25th November is surely not coincidentally related to John's release from prison little more than a fortnight later. Andrew Marvell was now Member of Parliament for Hull and, despite his previous associations with the Commonwealth, a Pro-Restorationist. Marvell publicly addressed a case for pardoning Milton that was for some self-evident. He pointed out that Milton had become blind so shortly after the execution of the king, that this was God's retributionary strike against a good man who had been led astray by politicians and that he should be left to endure and reflect upon this righteous punishment.

Marvell's presenting of Milton's condition to his accusers was both accurate and calculatedly selective. Milton had indeed endured circumstances that might be regarded as punitive:

a blind man dependent continually upon his friends and family being led, probably in disguise, from one hiding place to another. However, Marvell's characterisation of him as repentant and submissive was, to say the least, sympathetically biased. In March 1660, weeks before Monck brought his army south to meet the new King, Milton had published a pamphlet called the *Ready and Easy Way to Establish a Free Commonwealth*, a document which forcefully reiterated his arguments from ten years before, for a republic, and made clear that he regarded the imminent reinstitution of a monarch as disastrous for the state of the nation. The pamphlet was heroic and potentially suicidal in that Milton was aware that it would have no effect upon what was about to happen. Marvell's plea for tolerance, to those who would most certainly have been aware of Milton's pamphlet, was obviously a masterpiece of persuasive rhetoric.

For two years following Milton's release, the reprisals continued. As he went about London Milton must sometimes have found his blindness to be a solace. Regularly, those he had known well were being publicly executed. Samuel Pepys, in 1662, offers us a characteristically incurious description of a typical day.

> This morning before we sat, I went to Allgate; and at the Corner Shop, a drapers, I stood and did see Barkestead, Okey, and Corbet drawne toward the gallows at Tiburne; and there they were hanged and Quarterd. They all looked very cheerfully. But I hear they all die defending what they did to the King to be just – which is very strange. So to the office. And then home to dinner. (II, p. 66–7)

The last fourteen years of Milton's life, after his release in 1660, are treated economically by most of his biographers, because little happened, at least in the sense that he was no longer part of the political life of his country. His career as a pamphleteer was over, almost. In 1673, a year before his death, he returned briefly to the practice with *Of True Religion, Heresy,*

Schism, Toleration, and what best means may be used against the growth of Popery, which we will deal with later.

In 1663 he married again. Elizabeth Minshull (thereafter known as 'Betty'), a woman of decent, moneyed, middle-class stock, took control of the new household. At the time he was living in Jewin Street, in the parish of St Giles Cripplegate, part of the City. He had moved there a few years earlier from Holborn because the Jewin Street property had a garden. Now prevented by blindness from enjoying his long walks in parks and the countryside, unless accompanied, he made do with his own small expanse of land. It was probably for this same reason that he and Betty would move again in 1669 to a house in 'the Artillery Walk, leading to Bunhill Fields' (Edward Phillips: Darbishire, p. 75). Still in the parish of St Giles, this property was on the boundary between the City and the countryside. The Artillery Walk had houses only on one side and the Miltons' was surrounded by a large garden. To the north and east were open meadows and Milton would spend the rest of his life at this address. His daughters from his first marriage had during the previous decade been looked after by their maternal grandmother but had now returned to their father's house: Anne (aged seventeen), Mary (fifteen) and Deborah (ten). The relationship between Milton and his daughters would become the stuff of gossip and scurrilous legend, little if any of it founded upon attributable comments by the women themselves. Frequently cited is the alleged statement by the family maidservant Elizabeth Fisher that Mary, on being informed that her father was to remarry, professed indifference and added that 'if she could heare of his death that was something' (French, IV, pp. 374–5). Stories circulated, after Milton's death, that he had obliged Mary and Deborah to read to him in at least eight languages which they did not understand and, when others were not available, to transcribe what, were then, his own almost equally obscure compositions (French, V, p. 109). Parker, among many, questions the authenticity of this story, noting that it is entirely incongruous with Milton's perfectionism as a linguist and stylist.

Jonathan Richardson, one of Milton's first biographers and his near contemporary (born 1665), counters the rumours of Milton's alleged sclerotic behaviour as a father. He claims to have met one of his daughters and while not providing her name it is likely that he refers to Deborah, who lived in London in the early 1700s and would have been only thirteen years his senior.

> As we are at Loss as to the Particulars of the Affair, What I have Suggested will I hope be Sufficient, Only let Me add, that That Daughter, who was Certainly One (if there was really more than One) that was Thus Serviceable to her Excellent Father in his Distress, Express'd no Uneasiness, that I ever heard of, when she gave Accounts of *Milton's* Affairs to the Many Enquirers Lately; but on the Contrary, spoke of him with Great Tenderness; particularly I have been told She said He was Delightful Company, the Life of the Conversation, and That on Account of a Flow of Subject, and an Unaffected Chearfulness and Civility. One Instance of her Tender Rememberance of him I cannot forbear relating. The Picture in Crayons I have of him was shown her After several Others, or which were Pretended to be His; when Those were shown, and She was Ask'd if She could recollect if She had ever seen Such a Face. No, No. but when This was Produc'd, in a Transport, – 'tis My Father, 'tis my Dear Father! I see him! 'tis Him! And then She put her Hands to several Parts of Her Face, 'tis the very Man! Here, Here… – (Darbishire, p. 299)

There is no particular reason why we should trust Richardson's account but we have less cause not to. He had no personal, political or religious affiliation to what Milton had come to represent and had no cause to invent the story.

The only major events of his remaining years would be the plague of the summer of 1665 and the Great Fire of September 1666: Thomas Ellwood, a Quaker, a neighbour and regular acquaintance of Milton, arranged for the family to take a property in Chalfont St Giles to avoid the former. The fire did not affect the Bunhill house, situated as it was beyond the City, but it destroyed the original family home in Bread Street. The loss of Bread Street might seem of no enormous consequence in the life of the poet, but for two reasons it was.

First, despite the fact that through the 1650s and early 60s Milton had produced very few poems his reputation in England and Europe, partly from his early literary works and subsequently his career as a political-religious theoretician, was immense. During the Cromwellian regime and the early years of Charles II European visitors to London would ask to be shown the Bread Street house, where the legend had begun. It became the iconic centrepiece for speculation: what, if anything, was Milton doing or writing now? Such queries testify to the veil of silence that covered Milton's activities following the Restoration: he was writing *Paradise Lost*.

Second, for Milton himself, the loss of Bread Street was a financial catastrophe. His income from government work had, with the Restoration, ceased; Bread Street was his last piece of real estate and in 1666 fire insurance as we understand it did not exist. With an irony that was both bitter and perversely appropriate he produced during these years a poem that would endure as the most widely debated in English literature and which earned him virtually nothing.

Paradise Lost

Paradise Lost was published in August 1667 by Samuel Simmons (Parker, cited on the 1667 title page, was his representative). Within two years it had sold almost 4,000 copies; it was one of the bestsellers of the century. Royalties, in the modern under-standing of a writer's percentage of sales, were not a feature of seventeenth-century publishing. The printer-publisher made the object and sold it. The writer was paid mainly in advance for its contents. By 1669 Milton had received £20, roughly one-tenth of his annual salary as a Cromwellian civil servant.

He would spend his remaining years in a state of relative poverty while being celebrated as a poet almost beyond com-pare. At the beginning of the poem, when he seeks the aid of the 'heavenly muse' in his great task, one wonders if he is already aware of the paradoxical relationship between what he was about to do and what he had already done, been and experi-enced. He had been at the centre of events that would signifi-cantly affect the history of Europe, its political and religious destiny, and his presence had been forthright, vocal and tangible. Now he was going to explain to everyone why we are as we are; the verse would speak for him and he, partly by choice, partly by circumstance, would retire into the background.

No one is certain exactly when he began *Paradise Lost*. The manuscript is by various hands, but so was everything else

Milton produced after the early 1650s; he was blind. Clearly it was related to some of the thinking behind *De Doctrina*, but he would continue to contribute to this peculiar work almost until his death and it would be wrong to claim that the prose work was a plan for the poem or that the latter grew directly out of the former. The draft manuscript of *Adam Unparadized* (held in the library of Trinity College, Cambridge) shows that at least as early as 1639–40 the fundamentals of the project were in his mind, but this was conceived as a drama and there are no verbatim borrowings from it in the 1667 poem. It is assumed by most scholars that he started planning and making early drafts for *Paradise Lost* in the mid-1650s, but that he gave his time almost exclusively to its completion in the five years between 1661 and 1666. This of course raises the questions of whether or how the events of these years, the 1650s and 60s, as perceived and experienced by Milton affected his treatment of the poem's central themes: the rebellion of Satan and his compatriots against God; their defeat; the creation of man; the Fall of man, instigated by Satan; and its immediate consequences – effectively the contents of the first book of the Old Testament, Genesis.

Wars between noble households over their respective claims to a title or piece of land were an ongoing feature of the medieval world and more recently religious difference had fuelled conflicts throughout northern Europe, but the English Civil War was different. It began as a rebellion against an undisputed head of state, a rebellion that was founded upon, in modern parlance, ideology; a combination of economic, political, philosophical and religious discourses. It resulted in the execution of a monarch who was regarded by himself and his supporters as God's secular representative, and the foundation, for the first time ever, of a Christian republic. The events of the Civil War were shocking enough but a more fundamental state of uncertainty was caused by the fact that they had no established theoretical or practical precedents; and Milton during the 1650s was one among many who attempted, with reference to religious doctrine and classical learning, to make sense of what was happening.

In the seventeenth century literary works were not, in our sense of the word, reviewed. Studied responses in print to *Paradise Lost* would have to wait until the 1680s, but we can make some confident assumptions about the nature of the early discussions Milton knew he would prompt. First there would be a question. The original story, the book of Genesis, was known to everyone, so why was Milton rewriting it? Moreover why, by turning it into an epic poem, was he asking the reader to compare it with Homer's and Virgil's pre-Christian pieces? Milton did not change any of the detail of the Old Testament narrative – if he had it would have been spotted by the government censor, and the poem would have been banned; it was not – but what he did was to make the participants in this narrative, and himself as its coordinator, speak in a way that was different from the language of the English Bible.

All of the imaginative, stylistic and rhetorical resources of English Renaissance verse were channelled into *Paradise Lost*, and more: Milton individualised and universalised them. Milton did not alter Genesis but he modernised it, so that its figures would become as real and immediate as those who had dominated the previous thirty years of English history. He invited, virtually obliged, his first readers to consider parallels, allegorical relationships between his poeticisation of the original story of mankind and a more recent one, but the particulars were tantalizingly uncertain. Was Milton's Satan Cromwell? Was God Charles I? Perhaps Cromwell was God's proper representative and the collapse of his project, followed by the Restoration, was evidence of how Satanic elements still informed the condition of fallen man? These questions, even now, are still unresolved.

Romantic poets, Blake particularly, thought that Milton empathised with Satan and more recent interpreters, notably Empson in the twentieth century, found that Milton's Satan was an anticipation of modern nationalism. Christopher Hill, a

Marxist, regarded God as a version of outdated, feudalist authoritarianism and Satan as representative of the newly empowered mercantile classes. Such detailed interpretations would not be publicised for at least a century after the poem's appearance in print but their essence would have been anticipated, experienced, by contemporary readers. The only evidence of this comes from one Theodore Haak who in the 1680s translated *Paradise Lost* into his native German and told a friend how, fifteen years before, London had been alive with speculation about what the poem really meant (Hill, pp. 391–2). Was it only about God and Satan, Adam and Eve, or was it also using them figuratively, as a means of examining a more recent Fall and its consequences?

What we do know is that, alongside the tragic, violent polemicism of the Civil War, Milton's early life would have played a part in his writing of the poem. The conflict between fundamentalist Calvinism and Arminianism – is our fate predetermined or is it a matter of choice? – is central to *Paradise Lost*. Did God, omniscient as he is, know that Satan would rebel and was he aware that Adam and Eve, when he created them, would eat the fruit? Or, having given all of them the gift of free will, did he respond to the unanticipated consequences of their acts? English politics of the mid-seventeenth century resonate through the poem but also, carried into it, we encounter the fundamental disputes of all Europe during the sixteenth and seventeenth centuries. Milton's tutor, Thomas Young, his father's Protestantism and its family history, St Paul's School, Cambridge: all of these formative experiences fed the uncertainties and questionings that characterise the poem. Aside from the resonant subject of the poem it should also be pointed out that in its manner it altered significantly the history of English verse. Before the publication of *Paradise Lost*, blank verse was regarded as occupying a middle ground between poetry and ordinary language. It was deemed suitable only for plays, where actors might sometimes adopt a grandiosity of speech but since they were simply actors, pretenders to grandeur, the words they uttered were not regarded as true poetry. Rhyme was treated as a necessary feature of English verse; without it the line, the defining feature of poetry, disappeared. Milton in his note on 'The Verse' (added in the 1667 first addition) claims that his use of blank verse in non-dramatic poetry will overturn all of these presuppositions, that he has for the first time created the equivalent of Homer's and Virgil's unrhymed classical epics. He set a precedent. James Thomson's *The Seasons* (1730), William Cowper's *The Task* (1785) and William Wordsworth's *Tintern Abbey* (1798) and *The Prelude* (1850) depend for their existence upon Milton's intermeshing of inverted syntax and the unrhymed line. Stylistically, Milton created a new sub-genre for English poetry.

The first twenty-six lines of the first book introduce the theme of the poem – 'man's first disobedience, and the fruit / Of that forbidden tree whose mortal taste / Brought death into the world…' (1–3) – and contain a number of intriguing statements. Milton claims to be pursuing 'things unattempted yet in prose or rhyme' (16), which can be taken to mean an enterprise unparalleled in literary or non-literary writing. He calls upon 'the heavenly muse' to help him 'assert eternal providence, / And justify the ways of God to men' (25–6). Both of these statements carry immense implications, suggesting that he will offer a new perspective upon the indisputable truths of Christianity. The significance of this intensifies as we engage with the developing narrative.

In lines 27–83 Milton introduces the reader to Satan and his 'horrid crew', cast down into a recently constructed hell after their failed rebellion against God. For the rest of the book Milton shares his own description with the voices of Satan, Beelzebub and other members of the defeated assembly.

The most important parts of Book I are Satan's speeches. In the first he attempts to raise the mood of Beelzebub, his second in command, and displays a degree of heroic stoicism in defeat:

'What though the field be lost?/All is not lost' (105–6). By the second speech stubborn tenacity has evolved into composure and authority.

> *The mind is its own place, and in itself*
> *Can make a heaven of hell, a hell of heaven*
> *What matter where, if I be still the same,*
> *And what I should be all but less than he*
> *Whom thunder hath made greater? Here at least*
> *We shall be free; the almighty hath not built*
> *Here for his envy, will not drive us hence:*
> *Here we may reign secure, and in my choice*
> *To reign is worth ambition though in hell:*
> *Better to reign in hell, than serve in heaven.*
>
> (I: 254–63)

While not altering the substance of Genesis, Milton's style would remind contemporary readers of more recent texts. Henry V addressing his troops, Mark Antony stirring the passions of the crowd, even Richard III giving expression to his personal image of the political future, all exert the same command of the relation between circumstance, rhetoric and emotive effect. Milton's Satan is a literary presence in his own right, an embodiment of linguistic energy. In his first speech he is inspired yet speculative but by the second the language is precise, relentless, certain: 'The mind *is* its own place... We *shall* be free... We may reign *secure*'. The arrogant symmetry of line 263 has turned it into an idiom, a cliché of stubborn resistance: 'Better to reign in hell, than serve in heaven'. The question raised here is why Milton chose to begin his Christian epic with a heroic presentation of Satan.

Milton initiates a tension, a dynamic that will attend the entire poem, between the reader's purely literary response and our knowledge that the characters and their actions are the prototypes for all Christian perceptions of the human condition.

The principal figures of Homer's and Virgil's poems are our original heroes. The classical hero will face apparently insurmountable tasks and challenges and his struggles against the complex balance of fate and circumstance will cause us to admire and to identify with him. Milton invoked the heroic, cast Satan and his followers as tragic, defeated soldiers, and at the same time reminded the Christian reader that it is dangerous to sympathise with these particular figures. Throughout the book we encounter an uncertainty that is unmatched in English literature: has the author unleashed feelings, inclinations within himself that he can only partially control, or is he in full control and cautiously manipulating the reader's state of perplexity?

In Book II members of the Satanic Host – principally Satan himself, Moloch, Belial, Mammon and Beelzebub – discuss the alternatives available to them. Moloch (50–105) argues for a continuation of the war with God. Belial (118–228) and Mammon (237–83) encourage a form of stoical resignation – they should make the best of that to which they have been condemned. It is Beelzebub (309–416) who raises the possibility of an assault upon Earth, Eden, God's newest creation. Satan, significantly, stays in the background. He favours Beelzebub's proposal, which eventually wins the consensual proxy, but he allows his compatriots freedom of debate, and it is this feature of the book – its evocation of open exchange – that makes it important in our perception of *Paradise Lost* as in part an allegory on contemporary politics. Milton's attachment to the Parliamentarians during the Civil War, along with his role as senior civil servant to the Cromwellian cabinet, would have attuned him very well to the fractious rhetoric of political discourse. Indeed, in the vast number of pamphlets he was commissioned to write in defence of the Parliamentarian and republican causes, he was a participant, and we can find parallels between the speeches of the devils and Milton's own emboldened, inspirational prose.

For example, *Eikonoklastes*, in which he sought to justify the execution of Charles I, is often echoed in Moloch's argument that they should resume direct conflict with God. Milton invokes the courageous soldiers who gave their lives in the Civil War 'making glorious war against tyrants for the common liberty' and condemns those who would protest against the killing of Charles 'who hath offered at more cunning fetches to undermine our liberties, and put tyranny into an art, than any British king before him'. For Milton, the republicans embody 'the old English fortitude and love of freedom' (*CPW*, III, pp. 343–4). Similarly Moloch refers to those who bravely fought against God and now 'stand in arms, and longing wait/The signal to ascend' (55–6). Charles, the author of 'tyranny' in Milton's pamphlet, shares this status with Moloch's God: 'the prison of his tyranny who reigns/By our delay...' (59–60). Both Milton and Moloch continually raise the image of the defence of freedom against an autocratic tyrant.

Later in the book when Beelzebub is successfully arguing for an assault upon Earth he considers who would best serve their interests in this enterprise:

> ... *Who shall tempt with wandering feet*
> *The dark unbottomed infinite abyss*
> *And through the palpable obscure find out*
> *His uncouth way, or spread his airy flight*
> *Up borne with indefatigable wings*
> *Over the vast abrupt, ere he arrive*
> *The happy isle; what strength, what art can then*
> *Suffice, or what evasion bear him safe*
> *Through the strict sentries and stations thick*
> *Of angels watching round? ...*
> > *for on whom we send*
> *The weight of all our last hope relies.*

(II: 404–16)

The heroic presence to whom Beelzebub refers is of course Satan, their leader. In Milton's pamphlet *A Second Defence of the English People* (1654) he presents England as almost alone in Europe as the bastion of liberty and he elevates Cromwell to the position of heroic leader.

> You alone remain. On you has fallen the whole burden of our affairs. On you alone they depend. In unison we acknowledge your unexcelled virtue… Such have been your achievements as the greatest and most illustrious citizen… Your deeds surpass all degrees, not only of admiration but surely of titles too, and like the tops of pyramids bury themselves in the sky, towering above the popular favour of titles.
>
> (*CPW*, IV, pp. 671–2)

The parallels between Beelzebub's hyperbolic presentation of Satan and Milton's of Cromwell are apparent enough. Even Milton's subtle argument that Cromwell deserves a better status than that conferred by hereditary title echoes the devils' desire to find their own replacement for the heavenly order, with Satan at its head. Most early readers of *Paradise Lost* would spot the similarities between the devils' discourse and Milton's, produced barely fifteen years before – which further excites the debate on Milton's intentions.

Among the modern commentators, C.S. Lewis read the poem as a kind of instructive guide to the self-evident complexities of Christian belief. Waldock (1947) and Empson (1961) conducted humanist readings in which Satan emerges as a more engaging character than God. Blake (followed by Coleridge and Shelley) was the first humanist interpreter, claiming that Milton was of the 'Devil's Party' without being able to fully acknowledge his allegiance. Christopher Hill (1977), the Marxist, is probably the most radical of the humanist critics and he argues that Milton uses the Satanic rebellion as a means of investigating his own 'deeply divided personality'.

Satan, the battle ground for Milton's quarrel with himself, saw God as arbitrary power and nothing else. Against this he revolted: the Christian, Milton knew, must accept it. Yet how could a free and rational individual accept what God had done to his servants in England? On this reading, Milton expressed through Satan (of whom he disapproved) the dissatisfaction which he felt with the Father (whom intellectually he accepted).

(pp. 366–7)

Book III begins with the most candid, personal passage of the entire poem, generally referred to as the 'Address to Light' (1–55), in which Milton reflects upon his own blindness. He had already done so in Sonnet XVI. As we have seen, before that, and before his visual impairment, he had in 'L'Allegro' and 'Il Penseroso' considered the spiritual and perceptual consequences of, respectively, light and darkness. Here all of the previous themes seem to find an apotheosis. He appears to treat his blindness as a beneficent, fatalistic occurrence which will enable him to achieve what few if any poets had previously attempted, a characterisation of God.

> *So much the rather thou celestial light*
> *Shine inward, and the mind through all her powers*
> *Irradiate, there plant eyes, all mist from thence*
> *Purge and disperse, that I may see and tell*
> *Of things invisible to mortal sight.*

(III: 51–5)

Milton is not so much celebrating his blindness as treating it as a fitting correlative to a verbal enactment of 'things invisible to mortal sight', and by invisible he also means inconceivable.

God's address (56–134) is to his Son, who will of course be assigned the role of man's redeemer, and it involves principally God's foreknowledge of man's Fall. The following is its core passage.

> *So will fall*
> *He and his faithless Progeny: whose fault?*
> *Whose but his own? Ingrate, he had of me*
> *All he could have; I made him just and right,*
> *Sufficient to have stood, though free to fall.*
> *Such I created all the ethereal powers*
> *And spirits, both them who stood and them who failed;*
> *Freely they stood who stood, and fell who fell.*
> *Not free, what proof could they have given sincere*
> *Of true allegiance, constant faith or love,*
> *Where only what they needs must do, appeared,*
> *Not what they would? What praise could they receive?*
> *What pleasure I from such obedience paid,*
> *When will and reason (reason also is choice)*
> *Useless and vain, of freedom both despoiled,*
> *Made passive both, had served necessity,*
> *Not me.*

$$(\text{III: } 95\text{--}111)$$

The address tells us nothing that we do not already know, but its style has drawn the attention of critics. In the passage quoted, and throughout the rest of it, expansive language is rigorously avoided; there is no metaphor. This is appropriate, given that rhetoric during the Renaissance was at once celebrated and lamented as a reflection of the human condition; we use hyperbole and figurative language as substitutes for the forbidden realm of pure God-given truth. And God's avoidance of figurative language reminds us of who he is and of our guilty admiration for its use by the devils.

At the same time, irrespective of his sparse unostentatious language, God as a figure leaves an impression. He is clearly unsettled: 'whose fault?/Whose but his own?' He is aware that the Fall will occur, so why does he trouble himself with questions of guilt? And why, moreover, does God feel the need to explain himself, to apparently render himself blameless and excusable for events yet to occur: 'Not me?'

No contemporary reader would fail to recognise here an issue that had dogged religious debates of the previous century, had indeed contributed to the disputes that fuelled the Civil War: predestination. And Milton asks other questions that had troubled debaters. If man's Fall was predetermined had not God decided on the fate of his creation? What kind of individual would deliberately do such a thing?

We are shown in Book IV Adam and Eve conversing, praying and (elliptically described) making love, and this vision of Edenic bliss is juxtaposed with the arrival and the thoughts of Satan. Adam's opening speech (411–39) and Eve's reply (440–91) establish the roles and characteristics that for both of them will be maintained throughout the poem. Adam, created first, is the relatively experienced, wise figure of authority who explains their status in Paradise and the single rule of obedience and loyalty. Eve, in her description of her first moments of existence, discloses a less certain, perhaps impulsive, command of events and impressions.

> *That day I oft remember, when from sleep*
> *I first awaked, and found myself reposed*
> *Under a shade of flowers, much wondering where*
> *And what I was, whence thither brought, and how.*
> *Not distant far from thence a murmuring sound*
> *Of waters issued from a cave and spread*
> *Into a liquid plain, then stood unmoved*
> *Pure as the expanse of heaven; I thither went*
> *With unexperienced thought, and laid me down*
> *On the green bank, to look into the clear*
> *Smooth lake, that to me seemed another sky.*
> *As I bent down to look just opposite*
> *A shape within the watery gleam appeared*
> *Bending to look on me; I started back,*
> *It started back, but pleased I soon returned,*
> *Pleased it returned as soon with answering looks*

Of sympathy and love; there I had fixed
Mine eyes till now, and pined with vain desire,
Had not a voice thus warned me, What thou seest,
What there thou seest fair creature is thyself,
With thee it came and goes: but follow me,
And I will bring thee where no shadow stays
They coming, and thy soft embraces, he
Whose image thou art, him thou shall enjoy
Inseparably thine, to him shalt bear
Multitudes like thyself, and then be called
Mother of human race: what could I do,
But follow straight, invisibly thus led?
Till I espied thee.

(IV: 449–77)

Eve's attraction to her own image in the water is a straight-forward, indeed candid, disclosure of narcissism. Her first memory is of vain self-obsession. However, before we cite this as evidence of Milton's misogynistic portrayal of Eve, as by virtue of her gender the prototypical cause of the Fall, we should look more closely at the complexities of her speech.

For example, when she tells of looking 'into the clear/ Smooth lake' (458–9) she is performing a subtle balancing act between hesitation and a more confident command of her words. 'Clear' in seventeenth-century usage could be both a reference to clarity of vision ('*the* clear') and be used in its more conventional adjectival sense ('clear smooth lake'). Similarly with 'no shadow stays/Thy coming' (470–1), the implied pause after 'stays' could suggest it first as meaning 'prevents' and then in its less familiar sense of 'awaits'. Is she tentatively feeling her way through the traps and complexities of grammar, as would befit her ingenuous, unsophisticated state as someone recently introduced to language and perception? Or is Milton urging us to perceive her as, from her earliest moments, a rather cunning actress and natural rhetorician, someone who can use language as a means of presenting herself as touchingly naive and blameless in her instincts?

The issue is further complicated by the parallels between this episode and the remaining records of Milton's own life. We shall never know if he expected that later scholars would scrutinise this material and discover links and clues he had deliberately sewn into the texts but one cannot help sensing in Eve's disclosure of her narcissistic tendencies an echo of a letter that Milton sent to Diodati in November 1637. Ostensibly, he strives to inform his friend of where precisely his years of comfortable private study were leading him yet throughout he betrays something close to a confession to himself. He appears obsessed with neo-Platonic notions of beauty and while he does not quite allow that his 'vehement love for the beautiful' is self-directed, it would take only a small shift of nuance for him to become a version of Eve.

> Know that I cannot help loving people like you. For though I do not know what else God may have decreed for me, this certainly is true: He has instilled into me, if into anyone, a vehement love of the beautiful. Not so diligently is Ceres, according to the Fables, said to have sought her daughter Proserpina, as I seek for this idea of the beautiful, as if for some glorious image, throughout all the shapes and forms of things... Whence it happens that if I find anywhere one who, despising the warped judgement of the public, dares to feel and speak and be that which the greatest wisdom throughout all ages has taught to be best, I shall cling to him immediately from a kind of necessity. But if I, whether by nature or by my fate, am so equipped that I can by no effort and labor of mine rise to such glory and height of fame, still, I think that neither men nor Gods forbid me to reverence and honor those who have attained that glory or who are successfully aspiring to it. (*CPW*, I, pp. 326–7)

Satan, in reptilian disguise, is watching and listening to Eve, and Milton has him disclose his thoughts.

> *All is not theirs it seems:*
> *One fatal tree there stands of knowledge called,*
> *Forbidden them to taste: knowledge forbidden?*
> *Suspicious, reasonless. Why should their Lord*
> *Envy them that? Can it be sin to know,*
> *Can it be death? And do they only stand*
> *By ignorance, is that their happy state,*
> *The proof of their obedience and their faith?*
> *O fair foundation laid whereon to build*
> *Their ruin! Hence I will excite their minds*
> *With more desire to know...*

(IV: 513–24)

Without actually causing us to question the accepted facts regarding Satan's malicious, destructive intent Milton again prompts the reader to empathise with his thoughts – and speculations. Satan touches upon issues that would strike deeply into the mindset of the sophisticated Renaissance reader. Can there, should there, be limits to human knowledge? By asking questions about God's will and his design of the universe do we overreach ourselves? More significantly, was the original act of overreaching and its consequences – the eating of the fruit from the tree of knowledge as an aspiration to knowledge – intended by God as a warning?

All of the principal figures – Satan, God, Adam and Eve – have been caused to affect us in ways that we would associate as much with literary characterisation as with their functions within religious belief; they have been variously humanised. In *De Doctrina Christiana*, begun, it is assumed, only a few years before he started *Paradise Lost*, we encounter what could be regarded as the theological counterparts to the complex questions addressed in the poem. In a passage on predestination, one of the most contentious topics of the post-Reformation debate, Milton is, to say the least, challenging:

> Everyone agrees that man could have avoided falling. But if, because of God's decree, man could not help but fall (and the two contradictory opinions are sometimes voiced by the same people), then God's restoration of fallen man was a matter of justice not grace. For once it is granted that man fell, though not unwillingly, yet by necessity, it will always seem that necessity either prevailed upon his will by some secret influence, or else guided his will in some way. But if God foresaw that man would fall of his own accord, then there was no need for him to make a decree about the fall, but only about what would become of man who was going to fall. Since, then, God's supreme wisdom foreknew that first man's falling away, but did not decree it, it follows that, before the fall of man, predestination was not absolutely decreed either. Predestination, even after the fall, should always be considered and defined not so much the result of an actual decree but as arising from the immutable condition of a decree.

> (*CPW*, VI, p. 174)

If after reading this you feel rather more perplexed and uncertain about our understanding of God and the Fall than you did before, you are not alone. It is like being led blindfold through a maze. You start with a feeling of relative certainty about where you are and what surrounds you, and you end the journey with a sense of having returned to this state, but you are slightly troubled about where you've been in the meantime. Can we wrest an argument or a straightforward message from this passage? It would seem that predestination is, just like every other component of our conceptual universe, a result of the Fall. Thus, although God knew that man would fall, he did not cause (predetermine) the act of disobedience. As such, this is fairly orthodox theology, but in making his point Milton allows himself and his readers to stray into areas of paradox and doubt that seem to run against the overarching sense of certainty. For instance, he conceded that 'it will always seem that necessity either prevailed upon his [man's] will by some secret influence, or else guided his will in some way'. Milton admits here that man will never be able to prevent himself ('it will always seem') from wondering what actually caused Adam and Eve to eat the fruit. Was it fate, the influence of Satan, or Adam or Eve's own temperamental defects?

The passage certainly does not resolve the uncertainties encountered in the first four books, but it does present itself as a curious mirror-image of the poem. Just as in the poem the immutable doctrine of scripture sits uneasily with the disorientating complexities of literary writing, so our trust in theology will always be compromised by our urge to ask troubling questions. Considering these similarities it is possible to wonder if Milton decided to dramatize Genesis in order to throw into the foreground the very human tendencies of scepticism and self-doubt that exist only in the margins of conventional religious and philosophic thought. If so, why? As a form of personal catharsis, as an encoded manifesto for potential anti-Christianity, or as a means of revealing to readers the true depths of their uncertainties?

At the beginning of Book V God again becomes a speaking presence, stating that he despatches Raphael to 'render man inexcusable... Lest wilfully transgressing he present/Surprisal, unadmonished, unforewarned' (244–5). Line 244 offers a beautiful example of tactical ambiguity. Does 'Lest' refer to man's act of 'transgressing'? If so, we are caused again to consider the uneasy relation between free will, predestination and God's state of omniscience: surely God knows that man will transgress. Or does 'Lest' relate, less problematically, to man's potential reaction to the consequences of his act? Once more the reader is faced with the difficult choice between an acceptance of his limited knowledge of God's state and the presentation of God as a humanised literary character.

The arrival of Raphael (V: 308–576) brings with it a number of intriguing, often troubling, issues. Food plays a significant part. Eve is busy preparing a meal for their first guest.

She turns, on hospitable thoughts intent
What choice to choose for delicacy best,
What order so contrived as not to mix
Tastes, not well-joined, inelegant, but bring
Taste after taste upheld with kindliest change.

(V: 332–6)

This passage might seem to be an innocuous digression on the domestic bliss of the newlyweds – with Eve presented as a Restoration prototype for Mrs Beeton or Nigella Lawson – but there are serious resonances. For one thing her hesitant, anxious state of mind appears to confirm the conventional, male, social and psychological model of 'female' behaviour – should we then be surprised that she will be the first to transgress, given her limitations? Also, the passage is a fitting preamble for Raphael's first informal act of instruction. Milton sets the scene with, 'A while discourse they hold; / No fear lest dinner cool' (395–6), reminding us that fire would be part of the punishment for the Fall; before that neither food nor anything else needed to be heated. The 'discourse' itself, on Raphael's part, treats food as a useful starting point for a mapping out of the chain of being. Raphael, as he demonstrates by his presence and his ability to eat, can shift between transubstantial states; being an angel he spends most of his time as pure spirit. At lines 493–9 he states that

Time may come when men
With angels may participate, and find
No inconvenient diet, nor too light fare;
And from these corporal nutriments perhaps

Your bodies may at last turn to spirit,
Improved by tract of time, and winged ascend
Ethereal...

(V: 493–8)

Raphael will expand upon this crucial point throughout the four central books: it is God's intention that man, presently part spirit, part substance, will gradually move up the chain of being and replace Satan's fallen crew as the equivalent of the new band of angels. How exactly this will occur is not specified but Raphael here implies, without really explaining, that there is some mysterious causal relationship between such physical experiences as eating and the gradual transformation to an angelic, spiritual condition: his figurative language is puzzling. It would, however, strike a familiar chord for Eve, who at the beginning of the book had described to Adam her strange dream about the forbidden fruit and an unidentified tempter who tells her to 'Taste this, and be henceforth among the gods/Thyself a goddess, not to earth confined' (V: 77–8). Later, in Book IX, just before she eats the fruit, Satan plays upon this same curious equation between eating and spirituality: 'And what are gods that man may not become/As they, participating godlike food?' (IX: 716–17).

Milton appears to be sewing into the poem a fabric of clues for the attentive reader, clues that suggest some sort of causal, psychological explanation for the Fall. In this instance it might appear that Raphael's well meant, but perhaps misleading, discourse creates for Eve just the right amount of intriguing possibilities to make her decision to eat the fruit almost inevitable. In consequence, God's statement that Raphael's role is to 'render man inexcusable' sounds a little optimistic.

Books VI–VIII are concerned almost exclusively with Raphael's instructive exchanges with Adam; Eve, not always present, is kept informed of this by Adam during their own conversations. Book VI mainly involves Raphael's description of Satan's revolt, the subsequent battles and God's victory. Book VII deals mainly with the history of Creation and in Book VIII Raphael explains to Adam the state and dimensions of the Cosmos. The detail of all this is of relatively slight significance for an understanding of the poem itself. Much of it involves an orthodox account of the Old Testament story of Creation and the only notable feature is Milton's decision in Book VIII to follow, via Raphael, the ancient theory of Ptolemy that the earth is the centre of the universe. Copernicus, the sixteenth-century astronomer, had countered this with the then controversial model of the earth revolving around the sun, to which Raphael alludes (without of course naming Copernicus) but largely discounts. Milton had met Galileo and certainly knew of his confirmation of the Copernican model. His choice to retain the Ptolemaic system for *Paradise Lost* was not alluded to in his *ex cathedra* writing and was probably made for dramatic purposes; in terms of man's fate the earth was indeed at the centre of things.

More significant than the empirical details of Raphael's disclosures is Adam's level of understanding. Constantly, Raphael interrupts Adam and speaks of God's gift of reason, the power of the intellect, and which is the principal distinction between human beings and other earthbound, sentient creatures. At the end of Book VI Raphael relates reason (563–76) to free will (520–35). Adam is told (and the advice will be oft repeated) that their future will depend not upon some prearranged 'destiny' but upon their own decisions and actions, but that they should maintain a degree of caution regarding how much they are able, as yet, to fully comprehend of God's design and intent. In short, their future will be of their own making while their understanding of the broader framework within which they must make decisions is limited and partial. At the end of Book VI, for example, after Raphael has provided a lengthy portrayal of the war in heaven he informs Adam that he should not take this too literally. It has been an allegory, an extended metaphor, a 'measuring [of] things in heaven by things on Earth' (893).

In Book VIII, before his depiction of the Cosmos, Raphael again reminds Adam that he is not capable of fully appreciating its vast complexity:

> The great architect
> Did wisely to conceal, and not divulge,
> His secrets to be scanned by them who ought
> Rather admire; or if they list to try
> Conjecture, he his fabric of the heavens
> Hath left to their disputes, perhaps to move
> His laughter at their quaint opinions wide
>
> (VIII: 72–8)

This is frequently treated as an allusion to the ongoing debate on the validity of the Ptolemaic or the Copernican models of earth and the planets, but it also has a rhetorical function in sustaining a degree of tension between man's gift of reason and the at once tantalising yet dangerous possibilities that might accompany its use. All of this carries significant, but by no means transparent, relevance for a number of theological issues with which Milton was involved; principally the Calvinist notion of predestination versus the Arminianist concept of free will as a determinant of fate.

Later in Book VIII (357–451) Adam tells Raphael of his first conversation with God just prior to the creation of Eve, which resembles a Socratic dialogue. Socrates, the Greek philosopher, engaged in a technique when instructing a pupil of not imposing a belief but sowing his discourse with enough speculations and possibilities to engage the pupil's facilities of enquiry and reason. Through this exchange of questions and propositions they would move together toward a final, logically valid conclusion. The following is a summary of its implementation by God with Adam.

Adam laments his solitude. God says, well you're not alone, you have other creatures, the angels and me. Yes, says Adam, but

I want an equal partner. God replies. Consider my state. I don't need a consort. Adam returns, most impressively, with the argument that God is a perfect self-sufficiency, but man must be complemented in order to multiply. Quite so, says God. This was my intention all along. And he creates Eve. As if to invite a comparison Milton places Adam's description of his exchange with God not too long before a similar conversation takes place between Eve and Satan, in Book IX, just prior to her decision to eat the fruit.

> *ye shall not die;*
> *How should ye? By the fruit? It gives you life*
> *To knowledge. By the threatener? Look on me,*
> *Me who have touched and tasted, yet both live,*
> *And life more perfect have attained than fate*
> *Meant me, by venturing higher than my lot.*
> *Shall that be shut to man, which to the beast*
> *Is open?*

(IX: 685–93)

Having raised the possibility that death is but a form of transformation beyond the merely physical, he delivers a very cunning follow-up.

> *So ye shall die perhaps, by putting off*
> *Human, to put on gods, death to be wished,*
> *Though threatened, which no worse than this can bring.*
> *And what are gods that man may not become*
> *As they, participating godlike food?*

(IX: 713–17)

In short, he suggests that the fruit, forbidden but for reasons yet obscure, might be the key to that which is promised.

Eve's reply to Satan's extensive, even-handed listing of the ethical and practical considerations of her decision is equally thoughtful. She raises a question, 'In plain then, what forbids he but to know / Forbids us good, forbids us to be wise?' (758–9) and expands, 'What fear I then, rather what know to fear / Under this ignorance of good and evil, / Of God or death, of law or penalty?' Adam and Eve have continually been advised by Raphael of their state of relative ignorance while they have also been promised enlightenment. It is evident from Eve's speech that she regards the rule of obedience as in some way part, as yet unspecified, of the existential puzzle which their own much promoted gift of reason will gradually enable them to untangle. They are aware that their observance of the rule is a token of their love and loyalty, but as Satan implies, such an edict is open to interpretation.

> *What can your knowledge hurt him, or this tree*
> *Import against his will, if all be his:*
> *Or is it envy, and can envy dwell*
> *In heavenly breasts?*

(IX: 727–30)

Eve's exchange with Satan inevitably prompts the reader to recall Adam's very recent own exchange with God and, indeed, his extended dialogue with Raphael. In each instance the human figure is naive, far less informed than their interlocutor, while the latter both instructs and encourages his pupil to rationalise and speculate.

Eve does of course eat the fruit, and during lines 896–1016 she confronts Adam with her act. Adam's response and his eventual decision to follow Eve are intriguing because, while the misuse, or misunderstanding of the gift of reason was the significant factor for her, Adam is affected as much by emotional, instinctive registers.

> *I feel*
> *The link of nature draw me: flesh of flesh,*

> *Bone of my bone thou art, and from thy state*
> *Mine never shall be parted, bliss or woe.*
>
> (IX: 913–16)

This is addressed 'to himself', and then to Eve he states that:

> *So forcible within my heart I feel*
> *The bond of nature draw me to my own,*
> *My own in thee, for what thou art is mine;*
> *One flesh; to lose thee were to lose myself.*
>
> (IX: 955–9)

And the episode is summed up by Milton:

> *She gave him of that fair enticing fruit*
> *With liberal hand: he scrupled not to eat*
> *Against his better knowledge, not deceived,*
> *But fondly overcome with female charm.*
>
> (IX: 996–9)

These passages raise questions about chronology and characterisation. We already know from Book VIII (607–17) that Adam appreciates that the love he feels for Eve (partly physical) partakes of his greater love for God (mutual and transcendent), and we might wonder why and how Adam seems able to move so rapidly to a state of almost obsessive physical bonding with her: 'The link of nature', 'flesh of flesh', 'The bond of nature', 'My own in Thee', 'One flesh'. Moreover, during Milton's report in Book IV on Adam and Eve's innocent act of sexual liaison we were informed that the base, lust-fulfilling dimension of sex is a consequence of the Fall, and this is confirmed shortly after he too eats the fruit and they engage in acts 'of amorous intent' (IX: 1035). It seems odd, therefore, that Adam, still unfallen, seems to be persuaded to eat the fruit by the post-lapsarian instinct of pure physical desire.

One explanation of Milton offering these puzzling, slightly inconsistent scenarios could be implicit in his own rationale of Adam's decision: 'not deceived/But fondly overcome with female charm' (998–9). From this it would seem that her explanation of the act of disobedience is of virtually no significance compared with the sub-rational power of attraction that she shares, or will share, with the rest of her gender.

Charges of misogyny against Milton go back as far as Samuel Johnson and are generally founded upon the biographical formula that the failure of his first marriage to Mary Powell was the motive for his divorce tracts and that these personal and ideological prejudices spilled over into his literary writing; it is worth pausing to reflect on this. Milton was a self-selecting but by no means easily manageable subject for modern feminists and Sandra Gilbert typifies the mood of the reproachers.

In a patriarchal Christian context the pagan goddess Wisdom may, Milton suggests, become the loathsome demoness Sin, for the intelligence of heaven is made up exclusively of 'Spirits Masculine' and woman like her dark double Sin, is a 'fair defect/Of Nature' (X: 891–2)... for sensitive readers brought up in the bosom of a 'masculinist', patristic, neo-Manichean church, the latent as well as the manifest content of such a powerful work as *Paradise Lost* was (and is) bruisingly real. To women the unholy trinity of Satan, Sin and Eve, diabolically mimicking the holy trinity of God, Christ and Adam, must have seemed even in the eighteenth and nineteenth centuries to illustrate [the] historical dispossession and degradation of the female principle.

(pp. 373–4)

According to Gilbert, women, both as readers and writers (she emphasises the work of the Brontës and Virginia Woolf), have been persistently shadowed by the presence of Milton's

Eve, the epitome of *naïveté*, gullibility, vulnerability and danger-ously unsophisticated caprice. She does not go so far as to blame Milton for creating this stereotypical image of womanhood but it is clear that she treats him as culpable in producing a literary monolith which endorses it. Others, such as David Aers and Bob Hodge (1981), offer a more measured assessment and compare *Paradise Lost* with the divorce pamphlets. They argue that on the one hand he promoted 'a revolutionary political and religious life which is also sexually radical' but that we shouldn't 'ignore Milton's inevitable complicity with orthodox sexist ideology... there are limits to how far even a heroic individual can transcend his background and education, in thought and practice' (p. 84). They conclude that *Paradise Lost* reflects his dilemma and that it is difficult to extrapolate from the poem a clear allegiance either to the sexist status quo or to the enlightened radicalism of the pamphlets.

Most modern surveys of Milton's treatment of gender are highly theoretical and treat him more as a symptom of some ideological mindset than as an independent thinker. An excep-tion is Edward Le Comte's *Milton and Sex* (1978). Le Comte con-tends that it would be absurd to pretend that Milton's private life did not influence his writing (Milton's several marriages are referred to) but he portrays him, convincingly, not as an embit-tered misogynist but as a man both confused and endearingly fascinated by the female state of mind. According to Le Comte, his dramatisation of the relationship between Adam and Eve provides a shrewd insight into the perpetual and self-destructive battles that accompany relationships between two people in love who do not properly understand each other; that is, most of us (pp. 94–100). Satan comes across as a kind of incompetent mar-riage guidance counsellor who confuses their misperceptions of each other even further. The dispute over Milton's convic-tions, or prejudices, on the matter of gender will continue but anyone who might doubt that he was a radical before his time should read *Tetrachordon*. He concedes that according to the Old

Testament men are regarded as having a closer resemblance to God than that between the almighty and women. However, Milton makes it clear that this should in no way be taken to sanction an endemic position of male superiority in marriage and society: 'man is not to hold her as a servant, but receives her into a part of that empire which God proclaims him to... largely as his own image and glory.' In marriage, 'if she exceed her husband in prudence and dexterity, and he contentedly yield; for then a superior and more natural law comes in, that the wiser should govern the less wise, whether male or female' (Yale, II, pp. 76–7). Milton could hardly have been expected to completely rewrite the biblical account of Adam and Eve, but he makes it clear in *Tetrachordon* that our relationships should be based on the acceptance of gender equality.

The narrative of the Fall is continued in Book X, with God observing the act of disobedience and sending the Son to pronounce judgement on Adam and Eve. The death sentence is deferred and they, and their offspring, are condemned to a limited tenure of earthly existence, much of it to be spent in thankless toil and sorrow (103–228). There then follows a lengthy section (228–720) in which Satan and his followers have their celebrations ruined by being turned into serpents and beset by unquenchable thirst and unassuagable appetite – so much for victory. The most important part is from line 720 to the end of the book, during which Adam and Eve contemplate suicide. Adam considers this in an introspective soliloquy.

> *But say*
> *That death be not one stroke, as I supposed,*
> *Bereaving sense, but endless misery*
> *From this day onward, which I feel begun*
> *Both in me, and without me, and so last*
> *To perpetuity.*
>
> (X: 808–13)

Adam is aware that self-inflicted death will involve a perpetuation, not a completion, of his tortured condition. This realisation prompts the circling, downward spiral of his inconclusive thought, until Eve arrives. She readily accepts blame for their condition. Adam is eventually moved by her contrition and they comfort each other. Crucially, the factor that enables Adam to organise his own thoughts properly is Eve's proposition that rather than kill themselves they should spare their offspring the consequences of their act and refuse to breed: 'Childless thou art, childless remain' (989). Adam points out that this would both further upset the God-given natural order of things and, most importantly, grant a final victory to Satan. He seems at last to be exercising his much promoted gift of reason in a manner that is concurrent with the will of God, which implies that reason is tempered by thoughtful restraint not through any form of enlightenment, but from punishment. This impression finds its theological counterpart in what is termed 'The Paradox of the Fortunate Fall', first considered in depth by St Augustine. The Fall is both paradoxical and fortunate because in the latter case it was a necessary stage in man's journey toward wisdom and awareness, while in the former it reminds us that we should not continually question and investigate God's will.

At the end of the book (1041–96) we are offered the spectacle of Adam and Eve no longer pondering such absolutes as the will of God and the nature of the cosmos but concentrating on more practical matters, such as how they might protect themselves from the new and disagreeable climate by rubbing two sticks together. Is Milton implicitly sanctioning the Augustinian notion of investigative restraint or is he presenting the originators of humanity as embodiments of pathetic, pitiable defeat?

In the two closing books, XI and XII, the angel Michael shows Adam a vision of the future, drawn mainly from the Old Testament but sometimes bearing a close resemblance to the condition of life in seventeenth-century England.

Adam is particularly distressed by the vision of Cain and Abel (XI: 429–60), the 'sight / Of terror, foul and ugly to behold / Horrid to think, how horrible to feel!' (463–5). Michael has already explained how, by some form of genetic inheritance, Adam is responsible for this spectacle of brother murdering brother. And we should remind ourselves that many of the first readers of this had memories of brothers, sons and fathers facing one another across English battlefields; indeed, the author's own brother was on the Royalist side.

> *These two are brethren, Adam, and to come*
> *Out of thy loins; the unjust the just hath slain,*
> *For envy that his brother's offering found*
> *From heaven acceptance; but the bloody fact*
> *Will be avenged, and other's faith approved.*
>
> (XI: 454–8)

The tragic consequences of a perpetual rivalry between two figures who believe that theirs is the better 'offering' to God might easily be regarded as a vision of the consequences of the Reformation. The specific description of war (638–81) pays allegiance to the Old Testament and Virgil but would certainly evoke memories of when Englishmen, barely a decade earlier,

> *Lay siege, encamped; by battery, scale and mine,*
> *Assaulting; others from the wall defend*
> *With dart and javelin, stones and sulphurous fire;*
> *On each hand slaughter and gigantic deeds.*
>
> (XI: 656–9)

One wonders if Milton's own experience of the Civil War, the Cromwellian Commonwealth and the Restoration, when death and destruction were perpetuated by man's perception of God's will, was in his mind when he wrote these passages.

Alongside the particulars of war and destruction Adam is shown more general, but no less distressing, pictures of the human condition. After enquiring of Michael if there are not better ways to die than in battle Adam is presented with the following:

A lazar house it seemed, wherein were laid
Numbers of all diseased, all maladies
Of ghastly spasm, or racking torture, qualms
Of heart-sick agony, all feverous kinds,
Convulsions, epilepsies, fierce catarrhs
Intestine stone and ulcer, colic pangs,
Demoniac frenzy, moping melancholy
And moon-struck madness, pining atrophy,
Marasmus, and wide wasting pestilence,
Dropsies, and asthmas, and joint racking rheums.
Dire was the tossing, deep the groans, despair
Tended the sick busiest from couch to couch;
And over them triumphant death his dart
Shook, but delayed to strike, though oft invoked
With vows, as their chief good, and final hope.

(XI: 479–93)

Disease, disablement, terminal illness and much pain will be inescapable and the only means by which their worst effects might be moderated is through abstinence and restraint: the pursuit of sensual pleasure brings its own form of physical punishment. Just prior to disclosing the 'lazar house' to Adam, Michael informs him that he is doing so 'that thou mayst know/What misery the inabstinence of Eve/Shall bring on men' (475–7) and yet again the reader feels troubled by narrative chronology. At no point in Eve's Book IX exchange with Satan does she even inadvertently disclose that hedonism plays some part in her desire to eat the fruit, but Michael clearly presents a causal relation between what she did and the self-destructive inabstinence of man's fallen state. During his conversations with Raphael, before the Fall, Adam might well have enquired about such apparent discontinuities, but not now because, as becomes evident in Book XII, Michael's instructive regimen is informed by, and apparently achieves, a different purpose.

Most of Book XII charts a tour of the Old and parts of the New Testament – Noah, the Flood, the Tower of Babel, the journey to the Promised Land and the coming of Christ – but its most important sections are towards the end when Adam is given the opportunity to reflect on what he has seen.

How soon hath thy prediction, seer blest,
Measured this transient world, the race of time,
Till time stand fixed; beyond is all abyss,
Eternity, whose end no eye can reach.
Greatly instructed I shall hence depart,
Greatly in peace of thought, and have my fill
Of knowledge, what this vessel can contain;
Beyond which was my folly to aspire.
Henceforth I learn, that to obey is best,
And love with fear the only God, to walk
As in his presence, ever to observe
His providence, and on him sole depend.

(XII: 553–64)

Michael answers, approvingly:

This having learned, thou hast attained the sum
Of wisdom; hope no higher.

(XII: 575–6)

While Adam does not specifically compare what he learns from Michael with his own state of mind before the Fall, he is clearly aware that the cause of the Fall was his inclination to 'aspire' to an over-ambitious, extended state of 'knowledge'.

The question that has attended practically all of the critical debates on the poem is encapsulated in three liens at the centre of Adam's speech.

> *Greatly instructed I shall hence depart,*
> *Greatly in peace of thought, and have my fill*
> *Of knowledge.*

(XII: 537–9)

The question is this: does Adam speak for the reader? And there are questions within the question. Did Milton intend the reader to share Adam's state of intellectual subordination to a mindset 'beyond which was [his] folly to aspire'? Are the tantalising complexities of the poem – the presentations of God and Satan, the intricate moral and theological problems raised in the narrative – designed to tempt the reader much as Adam had been tempted, and to remind us of the consequences? Or did Milton himself face uncertainties and did he use the poem not so much to resolve as to confront them?

Barely six years before he completed this passage, Milton, in hiding, would have heard that all his writings had been burnt by the public executioner. Yet he would have known also that this was more a performance, a display of wrath, than a comprehensive destruction of his work. The most hated pro-Cromwellian tracts had been hidden by erstwhile supporters of the Commonwealth and Milton would realise that at some point in the future readers would discover extraordinary and unsettling parallels between Adam's declaration of contrite overreaching, and defeat, and the closing passage of *The Likeliest Means To Remove Hirelings*, the treatise he produced when the daring experiment of the republic was about to be destroyed by the Restoration. The circumstances surrounding both utterances were almost identical: each man stood at the precipice of almost apocalyptic change and each knew that what they had hoped for was not to be.

Thus much I should perhaps have said though I were sure I should have spoken only to trees and stones; and had none to cry to, but with the Prophet, *O earth, earth, earth!* To tell the very Soil it self, what her perverse inhabitants are deaf to. Nay though what I have spoke, should happ'n (which Thou suffer not, who didst create mankind free; nor Thou next, who didst redeem us from being servants of men!) to be the last words of our expiring libertie. But I trust I shall have spoken perswasion to abundance of sensible and ingenuous men: to som perhaps whom God may raise of these stones to become children of reviving libertie; and may reclaim, though they seem now chusing them a captain back for *Egypt*, to bethink themselves a little and consider whether they are rushing; to exhort this torrent also of the people, not to be so impetuos, but to keep their due channel; and at length recovering and uniting thir better resolutions, now that they see already how open and unbounded the insolence and rage is of our common enemies, to stay these ruinous proceedings; justly and timely fearing to what a precipice of destruction the deluge of this epidemic madness would hurrie us through the general defection of a misguided and abus'd multitude.

(*CPW*, pp. 462–3)

I suspect that the weary resignation of Adam's surrender to intractable fate, sealed by Michael's injunction to 'hope no higher' was very different from what Milton continued to feel about the brief attempt to restore what was left of man's unfallen state. For Milton the dream had not quite died: 'But I trust I shall have spoken perswasion to abundance of sensible and ingenuous men: to som perhaps whom God may raise of these stones to become children of reviving libertie.'

For the remaining seven years of his life Milton's domestic and intellectual life seemed sanguine compared with the uncertainties and tensions of the previous three decades. Betty looked after the practicalities of the household and though she was by 1670 only thirty, half the age of her husband, the couple seemed temperamentally well matched. She had no knowledge of the classical languages but she shared his enjoyment of English verse. She read poetry to him and reported later that he liked best Spenser, Shakespeare and Cowley. She also seemed a skilled ironist: 'And being asked what he thought of Dryden, she said Dryden used sometimes to visit him, but he thought him no poet but a good rhymist' (French, p. 123). A true poet, she implies, must be capable of writing an epic without rhyme. She revived in him the love for music he had shared with his father. After dinner, that is in the mid-afternoon, she would sing while Milton accompanied her on an organ installed in one of the ground-floor rooms of the house in Artillery Walk. She was the source of the story of his being called upon by the court of Charles II for the use of his intellectual and rhetorical skills, and her pride in his reason for rejecting the invitation is clear enough. Milton, she reports, 'was applied to by message from the King, and invited to write for the Court, but his answer was, that such behaviour would be very inconsistent with his former conduct, for he had never yet employed his pen against his conscience' (French, p. 392).

Publishers, aware of the popularity of *Paradise Lost*, encouraged him to write more and he turned primarily to pieces that had lain in manuscript form for more than twenty years. *The History of Britain* went into print in 1670 and his book on thought and rhetoric *The Art of Logic* appeared in 1672. Each was learned and largely uncontroversial, and it is notable that during this scouring of old work for serviceable and profitable assets he chose to leave for the scrutiny of later scholars one of his most revolutionary prose works, *De Doctrina Christiana*. Probably, with knowledge of how his century would later be seen as a watershed in the history of England, he was planning for the future further revelations of a man, John Milton, who had been at the centre of these turbulent events.

But as a writer he had not quite retired. Two more important works would be produced.

Paradise Regained was published, along with *Samson Agonistes*, in 1671 and while there is considerable evidence that parts of the latter were composed as early as the late 1640s no one can claim knowledge of the state of this alleged first draft or, therefore, rule out the possibility of major revisions after 1660. In the Old Testament (Judges XII–XVI) Samson is presented as a folklorish giant, a figure with no special claim to intellect, while Milton's figure continually reflects upon and scrutinises his past, his condition and his future, seemingly attempting to find some rationale for how his acts have visited his present fate upon him. One could argue that in the late 1660s Milton felt himself to be in a situation not unlike Samson's. He had not like his hero been a military leader, but there are resemblances between the presentation in the poem of Samson as the robust inflexible symbol of the Israelite rebellion and Milton's role as the intractable defender against all theological and political assaults upon the Cromwellian cause. At the beginning of the poem Samson reflects upon his state.

> *Promise was that I*
> *Should Israel from Philistinean yoke deliver;*
> *Ask for this great deliverer now, and find him*
> *Eyeless in Gaza at the mill with slaves,*
> *Himself in bonds under Philistine yokes*

(38–42)

Substitute 'Cromwellian England' for 'Israel' and 'Royalist' for 'Philistine' and picture Milton reflecting on how he too had been imprisoned after his cause was defeated. In the early 1650s Milton's wife had left, if not exactly betrayed, him; but she had done so because of her familial attachment to the Royalist cause, and while his blindness had, he knew, developed as an illness many Royalists had argued that, like Samson, it was a divinely sanctioned punishment. Through Samson's exchanges with his father – a considerable variation by Milton upon the Biblical version – he emphasises that his various punishments are deserved not because his cause was unjust; but, quite the contrary, that they constitute his private destiny.

He imparts to Samson a sense not of regret, nor of despair; there is quiet resignation. He knows that what he and his compatriots had dared to implement would not be attempted again in his lifetime but nowhere is there a feeling of regret.

Paradise Regained is based on the New Testament story of the temptation of Christ by Satan in the wilderness (Luke, IV, 1–13; Matthew, IV, 1–11) and once more we are caused to wonder about Milton's motives in altering the Biblical version. For example, in Book III Satan offers Christ a potted account of attempts by human beings to impose their will upon an imperfect and disorderly world: Alexander the Great, Scipio, Pompey and Julius Caesar all feature. Those hungry for allegory might detect sightings of Charles I or, if otherwise disposed, Cromwell. We might speculate but Christ, after the display, will not even accept this invitation to comment on the ambitions and flaws of humankind.

> *Before mine eyes thou hast set; and in my ear*
> *Vented much policy, and projects deep*
> *Of enemies, of aids, battles and leagues,*
> *Plausible to the world, to me worth naught*

(390–3)

The crucial episode toward which the entire poem has been moving, occurs during Book IV lines 514–40. Satan finally speaks honestly of his state of mind, and the following passage is more frequently cited and debated than any other.

> *I thought thee worth my nearer view*
> *And narrower scrutiny, that I might learn*

In what degree and meaning thou art called
The Son of God, which bears no single sense;
The Son of God I also am, or was,
And if I was, I am; relation stands,
All men are Sons of God...

(IV: 514–20)

As line 520 shows, Satan has elected himself spokesman for the human condition and with this one gesture he and, by implication, Milton project the poem beyond its New Testament context.

This is quite a brilliant example of studied ambiguity. Satan at first seems contrite, humbly aware that his attempt to gain some insight into the temperament and condition of Christ was a hopeless endeavour. But rather than simply admitting to over-reaching his fallen condition he has come to the very different conclusion, that his initial impression of Christ as belonging in a very different realm is false; that he, Satan, should trust his own powers of reasoning and intuition because he and Christ share the same lineage: 'All men are sons of God...' If we are unclear about who else Milton had in mind when he created this image of vaulting ambition we should note that as he was completing this poem he was also preparing for publication his *History of Britain*. Much of this had been written during the 1650s but shortly before sending his final draft to the publisher he rewrote the most controversial part, the 'Digression' on recent history, particularly on the vainglorious behaviour of the Presbyterian clerics of the Westminster Assembly.

And if the state were in this plight, religion was not in much better: to reforme which a certain number of divines wer[e] called... [who] wanted not impudence... to seise into thir hands or not unwillinglie to accept (besides one sometimes two or more of the best Livings) collegiat masterships in the universitie, rich lectures in the cittie, setting

sile to all windes that might blow gaine into thir covetous
bosomes... And yet the main doctrine for which they tooke
such pay... was but to tell us in effect that thir doctrine was
worth nothing and the spiritual power of thir ministrie less
available then bodily compulsion; ... thir intents were cleere
to be no other then to have set up a spir[i]tual tyrannie by a
secular power to the advancing of thir owne authorit[ie].

(*CPW*, p. 447)

Like the Presbyterian divines, the Satan of *Paradise Regained* is
blinded by intellectual self-delusion. In both instances a specious
respect for the authority of the almighty disguises an abundance
of personal ambition.

While Milton was granted leave by the Censor to include
his opinions on the Presbyterians, the fact that he cautiously
avoided any reference to the execution of the king in *The History*
indicates that his continued existence as free man and writer was
conditional. He was entitled to maintain his long-held views on
religion and civil government but limited in what he might publish. He was not, however, completely absent from the continued, very bitter debates on the recent and present state of
England. In the summer of 1672 Milton's friend Andrew Marvell
engaged in print in an angry debate with the anti-non-conform-
ist Samuel Parker, the Archdeacon of Canterbury. Parker in *A
Preface Shewing what Grounds there are of Fears and Jealousies of
Popery* accuses the 'fanatick party' – specifically the dissenters and
independents supported by Milton – of 'fermenting' fear of invasion by Catholic powers as a pretext for undermining the monarchy. Marvell in *The Rehearsal Transpos'd* satirises Parker and
offers a vehement defence of the present king, Charles II's policy
of indulgence both for dissenters – including, by implication,
Milton – and Catholics. Tract followed tract during the debate
and quite soon the focus shifted from the nuances of contemporary politics to the question of whether Marvell was acting as the
mouthpiece for a figure whose anonymity guaranteed his safety,

his friend John Milton. The anonymous author of *The Transposer Rehears'd* contends that Marvell and Milton are co-authors of the defences of non-conformism and goes further, arguing that *Paradise Lost* is a subtle advocation of political and religious dissent. He cites as evidence for his case Milton's apparent rejection of the formal conventions of English verse. By employing blank verse Milton announces himself as a 'Leveller... a *Schismatick* in *Poetry... nonconformable* in point of Rhyme'.

He might have become peripheral to the centre-ground of politics but his presence had endured for those who remained committed to Cromwellianism and those who still sought revenge for what Cromwell had done.

Jonathan Richardson (1734) claimed to have received authentic, if sometimes second-hand, reports from those who knew him in his final years.

I have heard... that he Us'd to Sit in a Grey Coarse Cloath Coat at the Door of his House, near *Bun-hill* Fields Without *Moor-gate*, in Warm Sunny Weather to Enjoy the Fresh Air, and So, as well as in his Room, received the Visits of People of Distinguish'd Parts, as well as Quality, and very Lately I had the Good Fortune to have Another Picture of him from an Ancient Clergy-man in *Dorsetshire*, Dr. *Wright*; He found him in a Small House, he thinks but One Room on a Floor; in That, up One pair of Stairs, which was hung with a Rusty Green, he found *John Milton*, Sitting in an Elbow Chair, Black Cloaths, and Neat enough, Pale, but not Cadaverous, his Hands and Fingers Gouty, and with Chalk Stones, among Other Discourse He exprest Himself to This Purpose; that was he Free from the Pain This gave him, his Blindness would be Tolerable. (Darbishire, pp. 203–4)

Many witnesses state that he was severely plagued by gout, and that his possible cause of death by renal failure was associated with this condition. Among the visitors of 'Distinguish'd

Parts', it is certain that John Dryden, accompanied by fellow poet John Waller, went to Artillery Walk to request his approval for their adaptation of *Paradise Lost* for the stage and there were rumours – recounted by early biographers and grounded upon Betty's stories – that Charles II despatched agents to seek his opinion on how to prepare the organs of state for accession of his brother James, a Roman Catholic. The rumours are credible given that the situation that caused the Civil War seemed about to be repeated – and Milton, as one of the few who had survived that first apocalypse, would be a suitable choice to act as sagacious advisor to prevent a second.

According to Richardson (Darbishire, p. 203) Milton refused to become a complete recluse. One Mr Millington, a bookseller who had arranged the sale of much of Milton's library in 1670 – an indication of the state of his finances – was his guide during walks through the city and in the countryside near Artillery Walk, when Milton would wear a 'grey gamblet coat' of the sort favoured by Quakers, and more significantly carry a sword with a 'silver hilt'. It is unlikely that an elderly, blind man would be able to defend himself with such an instrument but it was a symbol of defiance: the defender of the 'old cause' had not quite surrendered.

His final prose polemic was written a year before his death. Wilson refers to *Of True Religion, Heresy, Schism, Toleration, and what best means may be used against the growth of Popery* (1673) as a 'dull little work'. There is good reason to disagree with his judgement. The pamphlet is short, fourteen pages in total, and if the careless state of the first editions is anything to go by, very hastily printed. All of this indicates that it was written and produced in response to rapidly unfolding events. Two months before its appearance Parliament had after an emergency session (ending on 29th March) passed the Test Act that obliged those seeking military or civil office to declare their allegiance to Anglicanism. It was clear who the Parliamentarians had in mind when shortly after the original Bill they passed an amendment called 'Ease of

Protestant Dissenters', allowing exemption for members of the numerous non-conformist sects. There was a growing fear that Charles II was planning to reinstitute Catholicism as the state religion. Catholics were becoming more active at court and the Duke of York, heir to the throne and commander of the fleet, was an outspoken supporter of the Papacy. In secret Charles II had signed a treaty with Louis XIV of France that at some point yet to be agreed French troops would play a key role in suppressing Protestantism in England. No proof of the existence of this treaty would appear until after Milton's death but rumours of other alliances between the two monarchs, including an open treaty with France for the invasion and occupation of Protestant Holland, led many to believe that once more the nation might soon be torn between the monarchy and Parliament. The Test Act was clearly a provocative gesture by the latter.

The Commonwealth was gone but for a short period Milton was prompted to revisit his role in it, this time as the defender of its legacy. In *Of True Religion* Milton makes it clear that the only true 'Heresy' is Catholicism and he absolves the often contradictory and sometimes bitterly divisive doctrines of the various branches of Protestantism as inevitable, and forgivably human, consequences of the pursuit of an ultimate understanding of the word of God. 'It is a human frailty to err, and no man is infallible here on earth. But so long as all these profess to set the Word of God only before them as the rule of faith and obedience… they had done what man can do.' He goes on to argue that the argumentative nature of Protestantism is the token of its value, allowing man to properly debate the nature of belief and existence. All of this involves, of course, an invitation to recollect the days when England was alive with dozens of radical theses, some proposing models for society that would not again be seriously countenanced until the nineteenth century. Milton makes it clear who the enemy of tolerance and free speech is. 'The Pope [Clement X] [who] pretends rights to kingdoms and states, especially this of England'. Compared with the merciless rhetoric of his pieces written in defence of the Commonwealth this one seems rather subdued, but its sense of calm betokens an equally undisturbed level of certainty and strength. The Milton of the 1650s is still there, resigned but unbroken.

Milton died quietly and without evident distress sometime between 8th and 10th November 1674. His estate, comprising goods, property, savings and investments, came to approximately £2000, but this seemingly considerable amount included a large number of debts still owed to him. His will, drafted by his brother Christopher, discloses a great deal about his feelings regarding a particular, very substantial, deferred payment and the same document would feed rumours concerning his relationship with his first wife and their daughters. 'The portion due to me from Mr Powell, my former wife's father, I leave to the unkind children I had by her, having received no part of it; but my meaning is, they shall have no other benefit of my estate than the said portion and what I have besides done for them, they having been very undutiful to me. All the residue of my estate I leave to the disposal of Elizabeth, my loving wife.' Eventually, a settlement was agreed through which each of the daughters was allowed £100, and Betty's generosity is thought to have played a part in this.

He was buried in the chancel of St Giles, Cripplegate. There was no great ceremony. Little is known about who attended the funeral: Betty and his daughters certainly – the will was read later; Marvell probably, but no one is sure. Edward Phillips describes him as having 'a very decent interment according to his Quality... being attended from His house to the Church by several Gentlemen then in Town, his principal well-wishers and admirers' (Darbishire, p. 76). St Giles is one of the few buildings in London to have survived the Great Fire and the Blitz. It has been repaired many times and its medieval bulk remains as a stubborn rejoinder to the soaring concrete and glass edifices that now cover the once peaceful parish of Cripplegate. Before Milton's death part of nearby Bunhill Fields had already been set aside as a burial ground for non-conformists. Bunyan and Blake would eventually be interred there. It might seem odd, then, that this champion of radicalism should choose an Anglican church as his resting place. According to Toland, 'in the latter part of his Life, he was not a profest Member of any particular Sect among Christians, he frequented none of their Assemblies, nor made use of their peculiar Rites in his Family. Whether this proceeded from a dislike of their uncharitable and endless Disputes, and that Love of Dominion, or Inclination to Persecution, which, he said, was a piece of Popery inseparable from all Churches; or whether he thought one might be a good Man, without subscribing to any Party; and that they had all in som things corrupted the Institutions of Jesus Christ, I will by no means adventure to determin' (Darbishire, p. 195). He dissociated himself from the practices of organised religion, and Toland's list of his probable reasons for doing so is consistent with what we know of him, but he never quite abandoned the spirit of Anglicanism, not because, like Laud, he saw the national church as the embodiment of a particular theological template; quite the opposite. He hoped Anglicanism, and England, would help cultivate diversity and toleration.

His mortal life concluded without much notice but he has lived on, perhaps more insistently than any other English literary writer, through the most turbulent periods of three subsequent centuries. Milton and Shakespeare are the two most important poets in English but the latter is a chimera. Apart from the fact that we know virtually nothing about the real William Shakespeare, our speculations concerning what sort of man he might have been are eclipsed by his performance as a magician with words. He wrote about everything and his fame is guaranteed by his refusal to reach conclusions on anything. Milton was Shakespeare's equal as a versifier and rhetorician but he excelled him as a literary tactician. Shakespeare enables us to rejoice in language's power to alter our perceptions of the human condition; Milton causes us to wonder what stubborn truths lie beneath the words. I could list all the major authors of Britain and America who have struggled, often bitterly, with the legacy of Milton's work and his enduring presence as a man, but it would be easier to cite those who have remained immune from both, a matter of single figures. A memorable testament to his significance is found, I think, in a work where one would least expect it. In 1969 Kingsley Amis published a very peculiar novel called *The Green Man*. In it, God appears in the twentieth-century sitting room of the drunken, lecherous innkeeper Maurice Allington, whose life has already been disturbed by a grotesque agent of Satan. Allington asks God why he continues to make life so hard for people, and God replies:

'No prospect of that, I'm afraid. Much too risky from the security point of view. I daren't take the chance of coming that far out into the open. Some of your chaps have found out quite enough already. Your friend Milton.' The young man nodded over at my bookshelves. 'He caught on to the idea of the work of art and the game and the rules and so forth. Just as well it never quite dawned on him who Satan was, or rather who he was a piece of. I'd have had to step in there if it had.' (Ch. 4)

Like Amis, his author, Allington is an erudite atheist who has to cope with the presence of God in a story he himself narrates, and for both to cite Milton as their precursor in such an enterprise is a considerable mark of respect. Here, and in *Paradise Lost*, literary writing is marshalled to deal with the fundamentals of human existence; Amis could choose only one exemplar. Milton still speaks to us. He still asks us questions about the existence of God, and, consequently, about how and why we treat each other as we do.

Biographies of Milton

Biographical accounts of Milton began to appear soon after his death, principally Aubrey (1681), Skinner (1687), Wood (1691), Phillips (John, undated), Phillips (Edward, 1694) and Toland (1698). Generally, these relied on three sources: interviews and word of mouth anecdotes; passages from Milton's own pamphlets in which he digresses into autobiography, particularly *The Reason of Church Government* (1642) and *Defensio Secunda* (1654); known but disputable accounts of seventeenth-century politics and the Civil War. Edward Phillips had a special advantage in that he was Milton's nephew and from the 1640s onwards his pupil and close acquaintance. His is the most cited of the early biographies, and, despite Phillips's occasionally careless deployment of dates and chronology, remained the principal source for most surveys before Masson (1859–94). Apart from Skinner, all of the above are reprinted in Darbishire (1932).

In the eighteenth century practically all biographical accounts were prefaces to collections of Milton's work, the best known being Richardson's (1734, reprinted in Darbishire), Birch's (1738) and Newton's (1749). These contained further material gleaned from interviews with surviving relatives and acquaintances (some questionable; see French) and began, with the benefit of retrospective distance, to consider causal relations between the life and the work. The most controversial and influential example of the latter appeared in the later eighteenth century: Johnson's 'Life of Milton' (1779). Johnson was an anti-Miltonist, partly because his verse did not attend to the ongoing conventions of Augustan writing, partly because of his radical, regicidal republicanism.

The Romantics' enthusiasm for Milton was mirrored in several sympathetic biographies, principally Hayley (1794) and De Quincey (1838), and this tendency for the author's affiliation to contemporaneous moods and trends continued to influence biography through the nineteenth century (see Ivimay, 1833).

The exception is David Masson's magisterial account (1859–94). Masson effectively initiated the second period of Milton biography in that while the early studies from Aubrey onwards were based on random, selective and often very partial commentaries, Masson collected and reassembled chronologically all available information on seventeenth-century history, literature and Milton's involvement with both.

Masson's twentieth-century counterpart is W.R. Parker (1968). Parker builds on and adds to Masson's fund of indisputable facts, but tends to give less attention to the broader historical and literary contexts – Parker incorporates all known and relevant written material and generally he uses these to attempt to tease out some semblance of Milton the man. His, so far, is the best life of Milton.

Most earlier twentieth-century biographies made no serious attempts to add to or challenge what was previously accepted; rather they offered fairly objective surveys for the contemporaneous reading public: Raleigh (1900), Belloc (1935), Hanford (1949), Bush (1964).

Since Parker, the three most interesting biographies have been Wilson's (1983), Levi's (1996) and Lewalski's (2000). The first reflects its author's conservative disposition in that he treats Milton as a kind of counterbalance for the late-twentieth-century state of dissolute, irreligious philistinism, while Levi's is the first comprehensive modern attempt to treat Milton's writings as a coded autobiography. Lewalski is good on Milton the writer and thinker, but not as good as Parker. Brown (1995) is more a survey of the literary, cultural and socio-political contexts of the life and work than a conventional biography. The shortest, most accessible and pleasantly illustrated modern biography is Wedgwood (1969).

Fletcher's *The Intellectual Development of John Milton* (1956) is, as its title suggests, a comprehensive survey of the philosophical, cultural and religious dimensions of Milton's life. French's *Life Records* (1949–58) provides access to the basic printed material upon which Milton biographies from Aubrey onwards have depended. *The Milton Encyclopedia* (Hunter, 1978) is an excellent reference guide for biographical issues.

Abbreviations and Referencing

Throughout the book, references to the works of Milton are taken from the following texts and abbreviated as shown:

TP   *The Poems*, eds J. Carey and A. Fowler (London: Longman, 1968)
CPW *The Complete Prose Works of John Milton*, ed. D.M. Wolfe (New Haven: Yale University Press, 1953–82)
TM   *The Trinity Manuscript* (reproduction: Menston: Scolar Press, 1972)
WJM *The Works of John Milton*, ed. F.A. Patterson (New York: Columbia University Press, 1931–40)

For the poetry, all references are to line numbers. For the prose works, all references are to page numbers. Where *CPW* or *WJM* are followed by a Roman numeral, e.g. *CPW* III, the reference includes a volume number.

For all other references, the Harvard system is used; full details of items cited can be found in the bibliography.

Bibliography

Aers, D. and Hodge, B., '"Rational Burning": Milton and Sex and Marriage' (1981). References from Zunder (1999).

Belloc, H., *Milton*, London: Cassell (1935).

Bloom, Harold, *The Anxiety of Influence*, Oxford: Oxford University Press (1973).

Bradford, R., *Paradise Lost. An Open Guide*, Buckingham: Open University Press (1992).

Bradford, R., *Silence and Sound. Theories of Poetics from the Eighteenth Century*, London: Associated University Presses (1992).

Brown, C., *John Milton. Sketch of His Life and Writings*, London: Weidenfeld and Nicolson (1964).

Danielson, D. (ed.), *The Cambridge Companion to Milton*, Cambridge: Cambridge University Press (1989).

Darbishire, Helen (ed.), *The Early Lives of John Milton*, London: Constable (1932).

Eliot, T.S., 'Milton I' (1936); 'Milton II' (1947), in *On Poetry and Poets*, London: Faber (1957).

Eliot, T.S., 'The Metaphysical Poets' (1921), in *Selected Essays*, London: Faber (1961).

Ellwood, T., *History of the Life of Thomas Ellwood*, London (1714).

Empson, W., *Milton's God*, London: Chatto (1961).

Evelyn, J., *The Diary of John Evelyn*, London: Macmillan (1908).

French, J.M. (ed.), *Life Records of John Milton*, New Jersey: Rutgers University Press (1949–58).

Gilbert, S., 'Patriarchal Poetry and Women Readers: Reflections on Milton's Bogey', *PMLA* 93 (1978), pp. 368–82.

Graves, Robert, *Wife to Mr Milton*, London: Cassell (1942).

Halkett, J., *Milton and the Idea of Matrimony*, New Haven: Yale University Press (1970).

Hanford, J., *John Milton, Englishman*, New York: Crown (1949).

Hayley, W., *Life of Milton*, London (1794).

Hill, Christopher, *Milton and the English Revolution*, London: Faber and Faber (1977).

Honigman, E.A.J. (ed.), *Milton's Sonnets*, London: Macmillan (1966).

Hunter, W.B. (ed.), *A Milton Encyclopedia*, 7 Vols., London: Associated University Presses (1978).

Ivimay, Joseph, *John Milton: His Life and Times, Religious and Political Opinions*, London (1833).

Johnson, S., *Lives of the Poets*, 1779–81; references from reprints in *Oxford Anthology of English Literature*, Vol. I, ed. Kermode, F. *et al.*, Oxford: Oxford University Press.

Kelley, M., *This Great Argument*, New Jersey: Princeton University Press (1941).

Leavis, F.R, *Revaluation*, London: Chatto (1936).

Le Comte, E., *Milton and Sex*, London: Macmillan (1978).

Levi, P., *Eden Renewed. The Public and Private Life of John Milton*, London: Macmillan (1996).

Lewalski, B.K., *The Life of John Milton*, Oxford: Blackwell (2000).

Lewis, C.S., *A Preface to Paradise Lost*, Oxford: Oxford University Press (1942).

Macauley, T., *The Works of Lord Macauley*, ed. Lady Trevelyan, Vol. 5, London: Longman (1875).

Masson, D., *Life of Milton*, 7 Vols, London (1859–94).

Milner, A., *John Milton and the English Revolution*, London: Macmillan (1981).

Milton, John, *The Compete Prose Works of John Milton*, ed. D.M. Wolfe, 8 Vols, New Haven: Yale University Press (1953–82).

Milton, John, *The Poems*, eds J. Carey and A. Fowler, London: Longman (1968).

Milton, John, *The Works of John Milton*, ed. F.A. Patterson, 20 Vols, New York: Columbia University Press (1931–40).

Muir, K., *John Milton*, London: Longman, Green & Co (1955).

Nicolson, M., *A Reader's Guide to John Milton*, London: Thames and Hudson (1964).

Parker, W.R., *Milton. A Biography*, Oxford: Oxford University Press (1968).

Phillips, Ed., *Life of Milton* (1694). References from Darbishire (1932).

Pepys, S. *The Diary of Samuel Pepys*, ed. R. Latham and W. Matthews, London: G. Bell (1908).

Raleigh, W., *Milton*, London (1900).

Ricks, C., *Milton's Grand Style*, Oxford: Oxford University Press (1963).

Rowe, A.L., *Milton the Puritan*, London: Macmillan (1977).

Spencer Hill, J., *John Milton: Poet, Priest and Prophet*, London (1979).

Tillyard, E.M.W., *Milton*, London: Chatto and Windus (1930).

Waldock, A.J.A., *Paradise Lost and its Critics*, Cambridge: Cambridge University Press (1947).

Wedgwood, C.V., *Milton and His World*, London: Lutterworth (1969).

Wilson, A.N., *The Life of John Milton*, Oxford: Oxford University Press (1983).

Wittreich, J. (ed.), *The Romantics on Milton*, Cleveland: Case Western Reserve University Press (1970).

Zunder, W. (ed.), *Paradise Lost. New Casebooks*, London: Macmillan (1999).

Biographical note

Born in Derbyshire, Richard Bradford was educated at the Universities of Wales and Oxford. He has written twenty-three books on topics as varied as eighteenth-century criticism and literature and the visual arts. Over the past decade, he has specialised in literary biography, his most recent book being *The Odd Couple. The Curious Friendship Between Kingsley Amis and Philip Larkin* (2012).

Praise for *First Boredom, Then Fear. The Life of Philip Larkin*:
'This book is easily the best on Larkin yet to appear... A great biography of a great artistic genius. Utterly magnificent.'
– *Daily Express*

Praise for *The Life of a Long-Distance Writer. The Biography of Alan Sillitoe*: 'Soaringly intelligent.' – *Daily Telegraph*

Praise for *Lucky Him. The Life of Kingsley Amis*. 'Traces the influences on [Amis]... with magisterial skill' – *Daily Telegraph*

Praise for *The Novel Now*. 'Clever as hell... a top notch survey.'
– *The Independent*

Praise for *The Odd Couple. The Curious Friendship Between Kingsley Amis and Philip Larkin*. 'Entertainingly related... with commendable brio... A fine critic [Bradford] gives due weight to the work, as well as regaling us with frank, sometimes scorching details of their lives.' – *The Spectator*

HESPERUS PRESS

Hesperus Press is committed to bringing near what is far – far both in space and time. Works written by the greatest authors, and unjustly neglected or simply little known in the English-speaking world, are made accessible through new translations and a completely fresh editorial approach. Through these classic works, the reader is introduced to the greatest writers from all times and all cultures.

For more information on Hesperus Press, please visit our website: **www.hesperuspress.com**